WAKE UP...
LIVE THE LIFE YOU
LOVE IN BEAUTY

OTHER
BOOKS
BY
STEVEN E

1994
Wake Up
An Inspirational Handbook

2001
Wake Up...Live the Life You Love
(1ˢᵗ Edition)

2002
Wake Up...Live the Life You Love
(2ⁿᵈ Edition)

III

2003
Wake Up...Shape Up...
Live the Life You Love

2003
Wake Up...Live the Life You Love:
Inspirational "How to" Stories

WAKE UP...LIVE THE LIFE YOU LOVE *In Beauty*

IV

WAKE UP...LIVE THE LIFE YOU LOVE

In Beauty

In Beauty

In Beauty

WAKE UP...
LIVE THE LIFE YOU
LOVE IN BEAUTY

By
Steven E
&
Lee Beard
and more than 50
of the world's top Beautymakers.

V

WAKE UP...LIVE THE LIFE YOU LOVE

Published by:
Little Seed Publishing, LLC.
P.O. Box 4483
Laguna Beach, CA 92652

Pre-Press Management by TAE Marketing Consultations
Robert Valentine, Senior Editor;
Katie Dunman, Associate Editor; Erin Forte-Wilson, Assistant Editor;
Adam Mathis, Assistant Editor; Jennie Crawford, Editorial Assistant
Text Design: Bob McLean

Cover Design: Anibal Fernandez

For information, contact Little Seed Publishing,
P.O. Box 4483, Laguna Beach, CA 92652, or phone 562-884-0062.

Distributed by Seven Locks Press
3100 W. Warner Ave. #8
Santa Ana, CA 92704

Library of Congress Cataloguing-In-Publication Data
ISBN: 0-9644706-5-9

$14.95 USA $24.95 Canada

For your free gift, go to: **www.wakeupand.com**

DEDICATION

The word "dedication" describes more than our recognition of those to whom this book is indebted. The word describes the commitment of Beautymakers throughout the world to their art, to their families, and to their clients and friends. They are dedicated to their continuing education, to the welfare of their clients, and to their dreams for a better life.

To these caring professionals this book is dedicated with respect for their skill and with appreciation for their selfless devotion to bringing out the inner beauty which they can see in each of us.

Steven E and Lee Beard

VII

How would you like to be in the next book
with a fabulous group of best selling authors?
Another Wake Up book is coming soon!

Visit: www.wakeupcoauthors.com

Additional author information can be found at:

www.wakeupcoauthors.com/beauty.htm

We would like to provide you with a gift
to enhance this book experience.
For your free gift, please visit

www.wakeupand.com

CONTENTS

For your free gift, go to: **www.wakeupand.com**

For your free gift, go to: **www.wakeupand.com**

XI

For your free gift, go to: **www.wakeupand.com**

XII

INTRODUCTION

Wake Up...Live the Life You Love In Beauty is the latest edition to the inspirational *Wake Up...Live the Life You Love* book series. In the following pages, you will find contributions from 50 of the world's top beautymakers. Each story contains personal accounts of triumph over physical, spiritual and emotional adversity. Each one shows how they overcame challenges to live the life they love. Also included are trade secrets and thoughtful beauty tips, submitted by the beautymakers, to enrich the reader's lives.

Most people go to salons or spas for a specific purpose: to get their hair styled, touch up their roots, get a manicure or whatever else they may need. Rarely do they say, "I'm going to see my hairdresser for counseling," or "I'm going to get my nails done so I can get something off my chest." The best beautymakers know that conversation, a nurturing tone, or just a listening ear is as important as the beauty treatment. Nobody knows better than these professionals that inner and outer beauty are tightly connected components of true beauty. When the client leaves the salon feeling confident, serene, and joyful as well as looking fantastic, the beautymaker knows his or her work is done.

The idea for the book surfaced two years ago when Steven E approached me about compiling a book specifically for and about the beauty industry. I have always thought it would be fun to write a book. Having a best-selling book was beyond anything I could ever imagine, especially with my hands full with my own salon, but before we knew it, Steven E and I began talking to and collecting stories from beautymakers. It was through this process that we met Michael Hall at a beauty event in Las Vegas. Michael saw the potential of this book making him a very valuable asset to this team. His unshakable faith and vision helped us through the completion of this work.

For your free gift, go to: **www.wakeupand.com**

Steven E, Michael Hall and all of the coauthors of *Wake Up…Live the Life You Love in Beauty* are certain that you will find these stories to be both insightful and informative. Not only will you have an opportunity to learn about the ins and outs of the beauty industry, but you'll also pick up fabulous beauty tips along the way.

You are about to enjoy a unique book that is the first of its kind in the beauty industry. The beautymakers made it happen and it has been an honor to meet and work with such a wide range of these stars. Their teamwork, perseverance and love is what made this book possible.

Oliver Nims and
The Beauty Makers

All coauthors are listed alphabetically
in the biographical index on page 135.

XIV

Reverse Your Age

Steven E

As young children growing up, we are molded physically, emotionally, mentally, and spiritually. As we become adults, it takes an immense amount of effort and energy to change our lives. We have the same life patterns and they are usually rigid and restrictive.

We have the same posture and body movements at work and at home. When we do a new movement or play ball with our friends or kids, our bodies experience pain. We say, "I must be getting old," when it would be more accurate to say, "I am experiencing pain because I haven't been taking care of my body."

When we stop exercising and stop taking care of our bodies, our overall movements become fewer and smaller. The saying, "What we do not use, we lose," is true. If you do not take care of your body, your connective tissue grows short, brittle, and calcifies. Your joints pull tight and become constricted. The combination of right exercise, such as Pilates, yoga, proper strength training and body massage, can help us enjoy a vibrancy and gracefulness throughout our lives.

When we take care of our bodies, we change old, stiff tissue through strengthening, stretching and massage. While tissues become invigorated and elastic, the awkward impaired movements become smooth and easy. Literally, you reverse the aging process of your body. A strong flexible body is the precursor of a strong, flexible mind.

Your body is always changing, renewing itself daily. Did you know that your stomach lining is different today than it was last week? It is brand new. Your skin is continually renewing itself as well. In fact, 90% of your whole body renews itself yearly.

The body is energy and is always transforming. What you may have eaten yesterday is part of your biceps today.

Our society is trained with the expectation that when we get old, we deteriorate. Just maybe, we get old in our thinking and our thinking makes us feel old. Stop thinking old and start taking action by doing things which make you feel young, vibrant and alive.

Beauty Tip: *The next time you experience a headache, or any kind of body ache, make sure you drink a few glasses of water, you may be dehydrated.*

Steven E
Creator of the #1 Best-selling
Wake Up...Live the Life You Love series
www.wakeuplive.com

2

The Eight Winds
Michael Hall

A few years ago I worked with engineers who had developed new technologies that had many applications in the beauty industry. As the business developed, I wanted to go full time with it. I had a full salon going and kept two personal assistants very busy. I merged my business with another salon and started giving my clients over to assistants and other stylists.

I had spent a year at this and literally "put up the farm." I became a multi-millionaire—on paper. Then the bottom fell out of the dotcom industry, and our investors started running away. I ended up losing my house, my car, and other "things" I had accumulated over my career.

With no where else to turn, I went back to the salon and started working behind the chair to build up my business all over again.

I scraped together money to buy a car, it lasted one month, bought another and it lasted two months. Got a third, it was totaled in a bad wreck on the freeway a few weeks later. I rode my bike, it got stolen. I lost my storage unit, fought through the creditors, financial headaches, domestic challenges, the legal hassles, and all the emotional and mental anxieties that came along. I kept recalling the words of Nichiren Diashonin, "A truly wise man will not be carried away by any of the eight winds: prosperity, decline, disgrace, honor, praise, censure, suffering and pleasure. He is neither elated by prosperity nor grieved by decline."

I had to persevere until I broke through. I knew that if nothing else, I could use this experience to inspire others.

Don't lose faith in yourself. Turn "poison into medicine." Whatever happens in our lives can be turned around. Use it to help others, learn and grow from it. If you do that, what was once a "negative" is now a benefit. Use the ground you fell on to lift yourself back up.

Consider life as three steps forward and one step back. The "back" step is where you'll catch your breath, gather your forces, and then you LEAP forward on your next step.

From my experiences working on fashion shows and my
"dotbomb" experience, I assembled a talented and fun team and
we're producing our own national hair/fashion shows with a
TV show in the works. I joined this book team as well and was
able to put a lot of people together for this book. Remember,
no matter what challenges you go through in life, 'winter always
turns to spring.'

Beauty Tip: *How to Stay Young*

> *Keep your mind open to new and different ideas. Look at*
> *familiar things from a different perspective. Don't be afraid*
> *to try new things be it foods, concepts, clothing, makeup or*
> *hairstyles. Re-invent yourself periodically and allow yourself*
> *to evolve. If you can do this, you'll always stay young in spirit!*

Michael Hall
www.Hairloungeandspa.com
www.fashionrocket.biz
michael@fashionrocket.biz

4

The Salon and Vietnam
Oliver Nims

2000 was the dawn of the new millennium – a year of change for me and many others.

July: I'm the owner of a small but successful salon in Orange County, California.

I can feel I'm ready for a change. My conscious mind thinks I need to expand my business in California; so, I contemplate buying a bigger shop to grow. I have my eye on two existing shops that are for sale.

Out of the blue, my friend Kelvin – going to Vietnam for a family wedding – invites me to go with him. He knows I'm a big fan of Vietnamese food, but this time I'm feeling hungry for an adventure! I accept.

August 15: I'm sitting at LAX waiting to board an EVA AIR 747, dreaming about what awaits me on the other side. Little do I know that this is the beginning of a long love affair with this country, its people, and the grub. My first surprise was Saigon – a little rough around the edges to be sure but completely vibrant, friendly, and full of life. Actually quite beautiful with it's French villas, growing skyline and lazy river running through it.

My second surprise was that I found a salon in town. Not a local "mirror on the wall, chair on the sidewalk" style place but a real salon with Goldwell color and a lovely well trained staff. The place was stylish, great atmosphere, and ready to employ a stylist from abroad, namely someone like me? ding ding

My 10-day vacation was over and I was back in O.C. but all I could think about was Vietnam – the balmy heat, the cold beer, and the beautiful, friendly women. The reasonable voice in my head said "play it safe, stay in California where you know the rules of the game, don't give up all you've worked for." My heart was pleading for me to go back to Vietnam; take a risk. Life may be long, but then again it might not, right?

As usual, I followed my heart. I sold my shop, packed up my stuff and by November I was living in Vietnam and working at "The Salon." Half my friends thought I was nuts; the other half wanted to follow my lead. Anyway, I haven't been the same since. I've been here 3 years and loving every minute of it. I have so many close friends here, and I'm never bored as there is always a new surprise or discovery right around the corner.

Another aspect of being here that gives me great satisfaction is the impact I have.

This is a big city with over 10 million people. The economy is growing so fast, but the beauty industry is still undeveloped, and the people here want the latest. I feel I provide at least a little of that here. A "beauty ambassador" if you will.

Most of all I'd like to thank Tam and Graham Taylor for providing me a lovely place at "The Salon" to work. It's an oasis for people to come beautify themselves and a place where I can do what I love to do. They are also riding the wave of growth here as they now have five salons in Saigon and one in Hanoi.

I highly recommend any hairstylist who needs a break, an adventure or just likes Vietnamese food to come for an extended stay. You will have a world class salon to work in while you make great money!

Beauty Tip: *Take a 3 week vacation to Vietnam. While here, get a massage every day, and a facial twice a week. Stay at a 5 star hotel; it will set you back as much as Motel 6 at home. Make sure to relax and be as lazy as possible but don't miss the beaches of Nha Trang, the waterfalls of Da Lat, and the ancient charm of Hue.*

Oliver Nims

The Salon and Vietnam

Graham Taylor

2000: the dawn of the new millennium; a year I spent searching for new talent and the right stylist. Business was booming and the demand for quality service from my customers was foremost in my mind.

I knew stylists were out there, but the opportunities in Asia and especially in Vietnam were almost certainly unknown to them.

I am not a stylist but I am the owner of a successful chain of salons in Saigon, catering mainly to the expatriate market, which my good wife, Tam, runs on a daily basis. We had four salons at the time and one more on the drawing boards.

I know the heart of the business is as always quality products and great service. Good service is a ready commodity in Vietnam, but quality stylists are as rare as hamburgers.

I wonder how to recruit new talent, hoping for some miracle. The advertisements on the Internet are not working. I consider the United States of America as a source of stylists and reject it. "Too much negative history," I conclude. The Americans that I had spoken with did not, for the most part, realize the war was over or that they had lost. I was used to brushing off questions such as, "Isn't it dangerous there?" and "What about the land mines and agent orange?" For such a large country, this very insular attitude seems a little incongruous. Maybe CNN is only watched by foreigners. I reverted to my usual focus of Europe and Australia from where most of our stylists had originated in the past.

It was therefore a surprise, in mid-August, to have the all-American, blond haired (dyed of course) blue-eyed Oliver walk through the door and ask if we were willing to hire a foreign stylist. It took a while, but by November, Oliver was on the floor, scissors in hand and ready for action.

The first few weeks are the test. Many stylists, being "creative types," are prone to impulsive actions. The sight of a leper on the street or seeing dog as a food source rather than a pet was sometimes too much to bear. Thinking more often with their hearts than their heads, they either loved Saigon or hated it. Invariably they were surprised by it.

Preconceptions about the place are generally far from the truth.

Bulgari and Louis Vuitton are available in their own flagship boutiques. Mercedes cars cruise the streets and high-speed broadband Internet access puts the entire world at your fingertips. Bill Gates is more famous than Stalin and communism has been reduced to a dirty word by the young entrepreneurial generation. The only thing that is difficult to find in this country is a seat in an English language class.

Stylists that make it through the incubation period find themselves reborn as the star of the moment. The guru status afforded them by their Vietnamese peers, and clients, elevates them to new heights. Almost without exception, the stylists rise to the challenge and excel in the business.

Oliver was no exception and, before long, commanded a broad and varied loyal customer base. For more than two years, Oliver was the star stylist of the expatriate world. He comes to visit sometimes, and we wonder together over a glass of cold Heineken, whether the grey matter between the American ears or the Pacific Ocean is the bigger obstacle.

Business still continues to grow in Vietnam and The Salon (opening its sixth salon next month) has continued to employ Australians, French, English and even Canadian stylists. Since August of the millennium year, however, there has never been another American stylist walk through the door.

The door is always open, and we do not even mind if our stylists cannot spell "colour."

Graham Taylor

If you think you could fit in then contact Graham Taylor at The Salon directly via E-mail; g.taylor@designtekgroup.org

Think Again
Ginger Boyle

At age five, while living in a small town in Wisconsin, I told my mother that I wanted to make people beautiful. I liked working on other people. Doing hair has been my joy and passion all of my life. I like to work in the moment, enjoying the moment but always moving forward.

I started out with nothing, and it hasn't always been easy. I would pick a city and go, always knowing I could do it. When you get through tough times and trials, you're always better for having had the experience. Sometimes, it seems like it's either comfort or pain. We want life to be easy; to stay in our comfort zone. But our challenges make us stronger. Striving to always be a student, I've always feared complacency.

Learning from Horst Rechelbacher, founder of Aveda Corporation (natural products with an intellectual and spiritual focus) was one of the best things that happened to me. Horst was a tremendous influence in my life with his "think positive" attitude. He was such a pioneer in the industry and such a driving force to help those around him to succeed.

I would like to teach and transfer that "you can do it" message to everyone – especially women. I want to see them succeed in a proper and professional way, not what we see portrayed as a Hollywood way to get to the top. Edith Head was a person that I always admired. Even up in years, she was continuing to make people beautiful.

At one time during my career when I had no money, I convinced a bank to give me a loan to start a salon. We went from a start-up operation to seven locations in one year. I held to the belief that when you think you can – you can. You have to have a strong desire.

When surveying my career, one of my greatest accomplishments is my marriage. It's a wonderful thing when two people can work together and support each other. My husband is a very skilled professional photographer, and we've been able to start a video and photography business where we could travel the world while working together.

If you think you can't do it, think again.

Beauty Tip: *If you really want it, dig deeper. Get a second opinion. You can do it.*

Ginger Boyle
hair@planetsalon.com

10

Opportunity is a Subtle Thing
Joe Siracusa

Every person has beauty. You are born with this gift of love and life. My mom "Jean" is a "Jeanius"- she is the magic person who taught me to notice the beauty in the world and appreciate the little things in life. I was blessed to have a mom like Jean.

My family had a retail business for 48 years that my grandmother and grandfather started. Big companies swallowed up our store right about the time I went to college. When I left home, I basically had my clothes. After graduating from The Drama Department at Carnegie Mellon University, I saved a thousand dollars, bought a one-way ticket to Luxembourg and took off to make my fortune in the world.

I began my quest in Amsterdam. On day three, a girl walked by. I noticed a small button on her lapel, RSC. I stopped her, and said, "RSC, that's the Royal Shakespeare Company in London. Do you know about the theatre here?"

She introduced me to some people in a pub. That evening I was asked to direct Sam Shepard's, *Cowboy Mouth*, and tour Holland. The tour was successful. My brother Marty, the best brother a guy could have, joined me overseas. We worked together for over twenty years and still do now. I was invited to direct at *The Festival Of Fools*, started my own theatre company, got a lead part in a Coca-Cola commercial and toured hundreds of cities across Europe for nearly ten years with wonderful people. I am now working on *The Hollywood Pro Series* with Eddie Foy III, the most influential casting director in entertainment. I am also working with Jerry Leiber and Mike Stoller (Leiber & Stoller, two of the all time great song writers, music producers and publishers of our time), and William Kotzwinkle, a best selling author on an original musical. I have lived a blessed life.

The beauty business and fashion industry came into my life in a similar way in Miami. Charlene Parson an icon and leader in fashion education and a truly remarkable person, brought me to fashion shows and introduced me to her world. I am a theatre

11

man. I instantly loved the fashion people – intelligent, alive, and very creative. They are beauty-full. I was "hooked" on this thing called fun. I began working for fun, and many important opportunities came into my life. I wanted to share the opportunity with everyone so I created www.fashionROCKET.biz, so anyone could have a chance.

Fashion is beauty. Fashion is art. Fashion is the architecture of what we wear. Fashion people work very hard to make one tiny fleeting-pleasing moment for all to enjoy. That is beauty!

Little things are the big things. Opportunity doesn't land on your life like a lottery ticket. It's quiet. It sneaks around. You have to find it. Opportunity is a subtle thing.

My name is Joe Siracusa. I love to entertain people. I created www.FashionROCKET.biz so anyone can have fun with his or her dreams and share the beauty that is theirs in the world of fashion and glamour.

Beauty Tip: *I have always been a positive person. My tip on beauty is simple; smile and always greet people with positive energy. No matter what the circumstances are when you smile, you will be more beautiful than you were a moment before. It's a small thing that doesn't cost one penny and it can bring you success.*

Joe Siracusa
www.fashionrocket.biz
joesiracusa@fashionrocket.biz

12

The Power of One Person
Bryan Durocher

Beautymakers are business makers. It's easy to think of beautymakers as givers—people who live only for others. But business makers need to think of self, too.

Everyone can use more positive reinforcement. Seventy percent of living to your fullest potential is believing in the unique qualities you possess. Your dreams will happen if you truly have a passion for them. The other 30 percent is putting your dreams into action.

We all need more positive reinforcement and clearer boundaries. Be selfish. How can you take care of anyone else's needs if you don't take care of yourself first?

When you go around pleasing everyone else instead of yourself, you end up pleasing no one—including you. Whether it is family, friends, co-workers, employees, or even clients, some people will never stop to consider your needs.

13

Define what will bring joy, passion, and happiness. This takes some thought to do right, when you please yourself first you will end up pleasing others as a side benefit.

Start your journey with a "vision statement." Write down exactly what your life would be like if there was nothing stopping you. What would your life look like? What would you feel like? How would you spend your time? Create that perfect schedule that suits your dream. Write about how your career will bring you passion so that you will be excited to go to work everyday. How would you spend time taking care of yourself?

Make it complete; don't leave anything out. Remember: In order to produce consistent extraordinary results they have to be defined.

We all have a purpose in our lives and it is up to us to find and fulfill that greatness. Imagine if everyone saw his or her greatness and put it to work! Don't wait for anyone else's approval to get started. If you wait for others' approval, you will be stuck in the driveway and never get onto the "road of life."

For your free gift, go to: **www.wakeupand.com**

When you take on a new goal ask yourself "does this make me happy?" When asking yourself that question you will start doing more of the things you like and less of the things you dislike.

Do not let your past or the perception of others determine what your life will be.

There is a great saying to guide our thinking: The past is history, the future is a mystery, now is the 'present,' and that is why they call it a gift.

Beauty Tip: *Spend five minutes a day working on your inner beauty and the outward glow you project will be better than any cosmetic you could apply.*

Bryan Durocher
www.durocherenterprises.com

14

Shampoo
Van Council

If you don't like who you are or where you are I've got good news for you: You can change!

I got off to a really good start in the foothills of the north Georgia Mountains, a great place to grow up. Everything was going great until I failed the first grade. School just got harder and they wanted to put me in the special education classes. I was a "slow learner" mainly because of a bad speech impediment (which turns out to be a good thing as a hairdresser because the clients think it's a foreign accent, and now I can charge more for my haircuts). The rest of my scholastic career was difficult; I slid through by the skin of my teeth.

It was my junior year of high school when I started thinking about what to do with the rest of my life. That was the year I saw the movie that changed my life: Shampoo, starring Warren Beatty. When I came out of the theater I was high and ready to go! What a perfect job! I would cut hair, get paid, and associate with beautiful women all day.

Living in a small town in Georgia, playing football, boxing, and being a typical girl-chaser made it hard for me to admit that I wanted to be a hairdresser. I was often the object of ridicule. I was a fish out of water, and to top it off, I was expelled from beauty school after 10 months. The owner of the beauty school told my mom that I was wasting his time and her money. I left, but my mom encouraged me to finish at another school. I took classes during the day, worked at night and had no money. But I loved doing hair.

When a woman sits in my chair, I can change how she feels about herself because I know that if she looks good, she feels good. I love that. I have the gift to look at a face shape or bone structure and to give that face balance. A great cut can give hair instant vitality and bounce; it can make thin hair look thicker, and make thick hair more manageable.

15

I can recall when one of my clients, sitting in my chair, started crying. I thought it had to do with the 10 inches of hair I had just cut off. To my surprise, she said she never dreamed her hair could look so beautiful. Inspired by her new hair, she was driven to make changes to her appearance. She changed her wardrobe and make-up, which gave her more confidence. The confidence led to a new career. Can you doubt that the haircut was the catalyst for all of those changes in her life?

Doing hair is not just about a haircut. It's about being of service to others, about doing my passion and working with my hands and heart to touch people.

Beauty Tip: *Quality attracts clients, and education creates quality.*

Van Council
www.vanmichael.com
reeve@vanmichael.com

16

Global Hair Domination!

Dean Banowetz

My whole life has been about the survival of the fittest. As one of a family of 15 children, you learned that if you're not quick enough, you don't eat.

I looked upon the Army as a relief. We lost my dad when I was 15, and the Army seemed a good way to get money for college. After active duty I tried art school at the University of Iowa, but my life didn't seem to have direction.

One day, my brother (sibling Nr. 12, Leon), an advertising agent, remarked, "You're a guy; you're creative; you'll do well with hair." As an ad agent, he knew both the value and the cost of a good haircut.

So, I enrolled in Bill Hill's College of Cosmetology. On the first day, I knew my brother had been right. This was perfect.

But I had to work and study at the same time. I had to build a clientele fast, and, somehow, I did. Right out of school Matrix Essentials hired me as a trainer. I started as a regional educator, then a divisional trainer, and then became one of their North American artists. Tuesdays through Fridays, I worked in my salon in Iowa; on the weekends I flew out to do shows.

I loved to work on stage, but I felt that I had to work twice as hard because I was from good ol' unfashionable Iowa. But in Iowa I had a salon; I had employees. What I needed was more direction.

I did some more training in California. When I returned, I had calls for my resume. One of my teachers suggested I apply for one job, "and I won't bother you again."

I applied to "Extra" and got the call. In two days, I had an interview. I arrived, prepared for a face-to-face talk. Instead, they slapped a brush in my hand and had me style the host's hair for 9 million viewers. Within two weeks, I was back in L.A. On Valentine's Day, 2000, I started doing hair for a nationally syndicated show.

17

The gracious Leeza Gibbons taught me about Hollywood. In the salon I am trying to help people, but in Hollywood, I'm building a relationship that is part of the image the performers have become. It's the relationship that is important. No matter that someone else might be able to duplicate the styling; they can never replace who I am. I love my clients. I protect them.

When I first met Ryan Seacrest, he said, "Do whatever you want." So I took a look, thought about what I saw and what I knew, and prepped his hair for flat-ironing. He jumped out of the chair!

"Sit down, "I said. "This is now about me as much as it is about you." Well, he liked what he saw, and I've been doing his hair for every show he's ever done since then.

Hollywood isn't Iowa, but caring about clients and developing a relationship of trust and reliability is the same on any coast; it's the same in any chair. Caring for appearance in television means caring about yourself and the people who depend on you. That's where we change lives, one head at a time.

Beauty Tip: *Winning isn't everything, but wanting to is. If you want to look good, you have to put the time into it. If you don't want to look good, you won't. You have to want to change internally, and you must invest the time, thought and effort to do it. You can't have your corn today if you didn't plant it yesterday. Study, question, and practice.*

Beauty Tip: *It's bizarre; people think I was picked up out of Iowa and dropped onto a throne in L.A. Regardless of your goals, if you have a strong work ethic it will happen. Nothing comes on a silver platter and, if it does, it's not silver. If you don't work, it's not going to happen. To handle yourself, use your head; to handle others, use your heart.*

Dean Banowetz
HollywoodHairGuy.com
Toluca Lake, CA

Making It Happen
Robert Cromeans

While working at a nightclub in Glasgow, Scotland, a large group of "Posers," cool-dressed people with style, would come into the club. They were hairdressers. Up to that point in my life, I had been restricted from individuality. So, hairdressing seemed to be a natural path for me.

Today, I speak to about 500,000 hairdressers a year about art, fashion, trends, career paths, and business. Whether for individual hairdressers or modern day salon owners, it is an incredible feeling to be helping others meet their individual goals.

Despite all the wonderful experiences my career has given me, the greatest experience of my life was the birth of my two children. Although they are both adopted, my wife and I were present at their deliveries. My hairdressing experience came in handy when cutting the cord. Being a parent is truly the best experience; it taught me the meaning of life. My son, Reed Heron, is now three and my daughter, Monaghan Rose, is two.

Many things during the course of life teach us. A few years ago, a friend of mine passed away from a heart attack in her sleep at only 37. She was an Olympic Gold Medallist, but her real accomplishments were her two beautiful children and loving husband.

Though the death of a loved one is tragic, there is a lesson to be had. Life is short, so, we must live it on a shorter time span. It is what I call the three to five year plan. Too often we build our dreams or goals based on retiring at 65. My advice to one million people is to accelerate the experience of life; to be more focused to obtain the things you dream of in retirement, and to make them happen today.

Obviously, I am not talking about money only, but spending quality time with friends and family. Time is the only thing that can never be returned.

Beauty Tip: *Appreciate everyday beauty; stop and smell the roses.*

Robert Cromeans

20

We Are Worthy

Melissa Yamaguchi

In our industry, gift certificates are sold heavily during the holidays. The two biggest holidays for us are Mother's Day and Valentine's Day. Without exception, the week after Mother's Day brings the most requests for refunds, usually accompanied by the comment, "I can't take this – my child needs…"

As women, we tell ourselves we are not worthy; we deflect and defer, and we avoid. We take second place to more pressing needs. I ask, "Who are we to not be worthy?"

Until we begin to fully believe in our value, how can we expect our children to value themselves or those in our lives to value us? We are inundated with a media-born image of the "perfect woman." That creature is the imaginary product of an eighth-grade boy's mentality.

Do you want the truth about beauty? You can't see it, but you can feel it. No amount of make-up or hair coloring, not even the perfect hair cut or perfect body, no fad diet, no injection of Botox, no make-over, nor any beauty treatment will disguise your anger, jealousy, cattiness, negative attitude, unwillingness to love, or your closed mind, heart or soul.

In order to allow the beauty with which you were born to surface, you must begin to breathe deeply and openly. You must begin to look with your eyes and your soul at your surroundings; at the people with whom you come in contact. You must begin to listen with your ears and heart and speak only with a kind and sensitive tongue. You must touch only with the spirit of God.

The essence of beauty is the focus on the generation of tomorrow, with our feet planted in the value of who we are today. Determine your virtues; define your views, and honor your values. Have the courage of your convictions.

In the words of Ruth Beebe Hill, "I own my life. And only mine. And so I shall appreciate my person. And so I shall make proper use of myself."

21

Beauty Tip: *Wake up with a positive affirmation of your day. Brush your teeth to immediately remove toxins. Dry brush your body to start circulation. Massage jojoba oil into your skin all over (include your face and scalp). Meditate. Exercise. Shower. Your skin will glow, your hair shine, your spirit soar.*

Melissa Chambers Yamaguchi
MCYama@aol.com

22

Life as a Daymaker

David Wagner

Living life as a Daymaker is like taking an expressway to spiritual enlightenment. There is no need to meditate for years, climb a mountain, or spend money on fancy, expensive retreats to find your true bliss. Just notice the people you encounter each day, and offer a small gesture to make their day. Give them the quality of attention that makes them feel important, smart, beautiful, or unique. It's nearly impossible to focus on your own problems when you're living life as a Daymaker.

I was working in my salon one day when one of my clients came in to have her hair styled for the evening. This was odd for her, since it was right in the middle of her usual five-week period between haircuts. She must have an important social engagement, I guessed. When she arrived, I asked her about her evening plans. "I don't have anything special going on," she told me. "I just want to look and feel good today."

I gave her a scalp massage, then shampooed and styled her hair. During our thirty minutes together, we joked and laughed. At the end, she smiled radiantly, hugging me goodbye. A few days later, true Daymaking pierced my soul. I received a letter from this client, now in the hospital. She told me she wanted her hair styled so it would look good for her funeral. She had planned to commit suicide that day. But she had such a wonderful time during our appointment which had given her hope that things could get better.

She went home and called her sister to take her to the hospital to get some help.

She thanked me for caring, even though I wasn't aware of her turmoil. I was stunned. I had spent time with this woman once a month for three years, yet I had no inkling that she was struggling with her life that day. I felt really moved that I had made such a difference for her. Still, it left me with an enormous sense of responsibility. What if I had been upset, distracted, or hurried when she came to see me? Would she have taken her life that day?

That experience made me take stock of myself as a stylist and as a Daymaker. How many of the ten clients I saw every day might be in a personal crisis that I would never know about? How many people do you know who have extreme challenges at any one time? You would have no way to tell who needed your help. I resolved to treat every person I met the way I treated her.

It might sound like a lot of work, but it isn't. It wasn't hard to have fun with my client that day. It was natural and made my day brighter, too. I thank her for the gift she gave me. My experience with her allowed me to see the difference I can make for others.

Why have "random acts of kindness?" Why not intentional acts of good will? Everyone can relate to Daymaking, and the ripple effect it creates has the power to change the world. Daymaking has no racial, religious, or economic boundaries, but the effects can be profound. One of us can significantly influence our community. It creates a tipping point in which the pendulum is biased in favor of kindness, care, love, and joy.

24

Beauty Tip: *True beauty lies in each of us, whether in a gracious smile or a helping hand. Spread beauty everyday, it doesn't cost a dime.*

David Wagner
www.daymakermovement.com

Finishing Strong During the Storms of Life

Lauren Gartland

The one thing you can count on in life is that adversity will happen. This is as predictable as the rising and setting of the sun. Each and every one of us will have troubles, obstacles and pain to overcome. It is not a matter of "if" but "when." The question that haunts us is what will we do when that time comes? This is my story about how I overcame the greatest storm of my life. May it give you hope and inspiration as you run your race, called life and give you the courage to finish strong.

In June of 2001, Randi Rose, the CFO of Inspiring Champions requested a meeting with me. Little did I know that this meeting would change my life forever. The first thing Randi said was, "I have good news for you and I have bad news. The good news is you have had a pinnacle year as far as revenue generated. You have exceeded your goals." The bad news, "Because you did not charge enough to cover the expenses of the Champ Camps you are in serious debt and in grave danger of going out of business." In that moment I had never felt such fear, hopelessness or desperation. How could we work this hard for six years and have it end like this? It didn't seem possible, and definitely did not seem fair.

The big question was, "What would we do?" Here are the valuable lessons I learned from this painful experience, which I hope will inspire you through your storms of life.

1) Grieving. With every loss there must be a mourning period. Whether it is the loss of a loved one, a broken relationship, a business or a financial loss. Any type of loss is painful, discomforting and can even be crippling. When you experience loss it is important to take quiet time to feel the pain and grieve. Cry, kick and scream until there is nothing left inside of you except a still voice that whispers, "Come. It is time to move on." Grieve but have the wisdom to know when it is time to press on.

2) Develop a spirit of humility. To avoid tarnishing my pride and ego by having to share what was happening, I simply chose to avoid the world and hide out. I needed to develop a spirit of humility and kill my pride and ego. Ego stands for "Edging God Out." It was time to take off the happy mask and admit that I needed help. It was a relief to finally let go of my secret and to begin responsibly sharing what was happening.

3) Learn to listen to your inner voice. One day as I cried out for help a voice inside of me said, "Lauren, what is success to you?" I was so shattered I did not want to explore the answer to this question. Then the voice said, "Lauren, if you measure your success by the numbers, by society's standards, you have not been successful. However, if you measure your success by the difference you have made and the lives you have impacted, in God's eyes you have been faithful and successful." By learning to stop and listen to my inner voice, the message I received set me free and helped me to let go and move on.

4) Ask for help! This for me is right up there with death by fire! My beliefs about asking for help brought up two questions: "Why would anyone want to help me?" And "If I ask for help they will think I am weak." This was the inner dialogue that held me back. When the tough times come, and they will, find the courage within to ask for help. In my own life, first seek guidance from God for he is our ultimate helper. He is wiser, stronger, more loving, more of everything than we are. Most often, we have not simply because we ask not.

5) Cast away your worries. Here is the most valuable but hardest lesson I had to learn.

Surrender! To cast away every worry, fear, concern and challenge and turn it over to something much bigger than me. One day, out of complete desperation, I got down on my knees and cried out, "God, I can't carry this burden any longer it is too much for me. Help me to move on." I repeated this until I felt complete peace in the greatest storm of my life. I have since coached many coaching clients, friends and family members during their trials and tribulations to do the same and each were amazed how it worked.

6) Soar on the wings of faith. To lose your faith during the storms of life is like letting go of your life preserver. Faith may be the only thing you have left to hang onto. You must believe that this will pass and from it will come great lessons that will move you forward to greater things. You can choose to fight and resist the storms of life or you can choose to fly through them on the wings of faith and know that like the majestic eagle you will soar above the storm.

Since this experience I have come to realize that every adversity and loss I have encountered has made me a better and stronger trainer, success coach and business owner. I have also witnessed the reinvention of our company and we are having our most profitable year ever. None of this success would be possible without the help of God and the support of my amazing team and our faithful clients. Without going through this, I would not be able to support and help people at the level I do now. There are no regrets! We are finishing strong!

Inspiring Champions serves salon professionals, who want to make more money, work fewer hours and live a balanced life. How we achieve this is through world-class business education and coaching. Our mission is to globally change the salon industry one professional at a time.

Beauty Tip: *"Beauty in Confidence and Courage!"*
One of the biggest fears each of us will face is aging. When that time comes remember this, "Years may wrinkle your skin but to not pursue your dreams will wrinkle your soul!" If you want to beautify your life find the confidence and courage to live your dreams.

Lauren Gartland
www.inspiringchampions.com
Lauren@inspiringchampions.com

28

Beauty Is A Life Long Journey at Avida Salon & Spa
Chris and Angie Freddi

This story is not just mine. It is the story of my wife Angie, our team and our wonderful community.

It all started about 12 years ago when I went for a haircut at a local salon here in El Paso, Texas, our hometown. El Paso is not exactly a Paris or New York, but it has its own particular charm. It's a wonderful, international, culturally diverse community with a tremendous amount of values and talent. Little did I know that this haircut would change my life; that this lovely hairdresser would someday be my wife.

In a way, El Paso is a lot like the many beautiful people we see everyday coming into our salon. They are culturally diverse, may have some rough challenges, but are simply diamonds in the rough, waiting for us to make that unique, unforgettable change in their lives.

While Angie and I were dating, the salon where she worked went up for sale and we decided to buy it. We decided to create our dream salon, always moving forward and never looking back, staying up-to-date with education and technology. In 1997, we invested in a computer imaging system so that clients could see themselves with different hairstyles. It became a big draw for new clients and an incredible tool to help people overcome their fear of change.

In the five short years that followed, we went from being an average four person salon to being rated among the top 200 salons in the entire United States by *Salon Today Magazine*! We did this by dreaming big and keeping faith in the dream.

Our Mission Statement Reads: "We are an all inclusive, collaborating force - Working and serving together to move our industry forward by showing the public that we are Beautymakers as well as professional business people."

We are so proud that our salon's photo shoot work has received national and international recognition and has been printed around the world. In 2002 we took a larger step and

29

started doing platform work at fashion shows. It has been a lot of work and pressure but ever so rewarding.

In June 2000, Angie became not only my business partner, but my life partner, as well. I am so proud of her. When Angie came to El Paso from Mexico she became a brilliant example of the American dream realized. She has had to overcome obstacles such as language barriers, leaving her childhood home and family, learning American business practices. Angie is a person with leadership, integrity, commitment, drive, professionalism and one of the hardest working people I have ever known.

In October 2002 we changed our name from Angie's Hair & Nail Salon to Avida Salon and Spa. We grew from 980 to 2,000 square feet. We went from four stylists to 12 and became a salon/spa with nearly every service you could think of, a full service salon and spa.

The word vida in Spanish means "life." I call Angie by the nickname Vida because she is my life. Since it is our life together, we came up with the name Avida Salon & Spa, which means "A Life" and with our salon here on the border it can be easily translated, giving meaning not only to our international friends, but also to those here in our community as well.

I knew nothing at the time about the awesome healing and feeling power that salons have and how they can actually influence and change people's feelings and lives, not to mention the ability to make someone look and feel incredible!

One of our regular clients disappeared for many months without a word. We weren't able to contact her and just assumed she had moved. About 5 months later the same woman came in one morning looking a little worn and without any hair. We found out she had been battling breast cancer for the last few months. We listened intently as she shared her story. We had the opportunity that day to really understand what it meant to be pampered with a massage, facial, manicure and pedicure. When we started to do her makeup, tears of joy rolled down her face as she told us this was the first time she felt really beautiful since she could remember. When she revisited our salon she told us that we had helped her wake up something deep within her; that if she felt beautiful inside, she would always be beautiful on the outside, hair or no hair.

Learning about our industry has always been a great pleasure for Angie and me. When we have the chance to visit other salons around the country it is truly a pleasure. From these great times we feel that it has helped our ability to see our dreams through the clouds. We want to encourage people in the industry to visit other salons, and make sure if you are ever in El Paso, please stop by and visit Avida's.

The real pleasure of going to work everyday is that we get to touch and be touched by the most wonderful people.

Beauty Tip: *Always visit your hairdresser. Feeling good is all about looking good, inside and out – and your stylist and salon professional are the ones that can help you unveil the real beauty that exists in you. And try to be a Beautymaker yourself. Always grow, learn, share and give back to your family, friends, co-workers and community. Make it not only a daily mission but also a never-ending lifelong journey.*

Chris and Angie Freddi
cfreddi@aol.com
www.avidasalon.com

31

32

The Beauty of It All

Norma D

I wonder how different life would be if I hadn't had a baby and gotten married at 16. I probably would have taken the traditional route; gone to college and worked at a good job only to be fired in the middle of a recession like the one we are having now. And then where would I be? Trying to figure out how I was going to pay the mortgage and looking for my next job.

Since my parents' plan for me was to go to college and get a good job, I didn't nurture the idea of going to school for cosmetology. The cost certainly would have been cheaper for my parents.

I went into parenthood as a teenager and believed that I was no longer worthy of a decent life with my peers. After two babies, two divorces and my last "traditional" job, I decided I wanted to do something that I loved no matter what sacrifices I had to make. I had complicated my life so much by getting pregnant that I decided it was time to make my life work. I knew I had to work, but this time, I wanted to do something that I loved.

So I quit my job that gave me benefits and four weeks vacation, and decided to attend beauty school in Livermore, California where I lived at the time, thinking I could get 800 credit hours there and then transfer to Oakland, 30 minutes away, to do the other 800 hours so I could learn how to do African American hair. As it turned out with life's twists and turns, qualifications changed during the late seventies and I had to finish in Livermore or start all over again in Oakland with no hours.

Looking back on how my interest in hair designing started, I can roar with laughter thinking how amazing it is that someone would pay me to do her hair. I loved to fool around with hair so much that I thought I should be the one to pay someone for letting me play with her hair.

33

I am glad that I was willing to do the things I needed to do to be happy working as a cosmetologist so that I could have the life I have today.

Live the life you love and the rewards will come, even if it is later down the road.

Beauty Tip: *Reward yourself.*

Norma D

34

Our Inner Script
Scott Duvall

Like most stories of inspiration and motivation, we need to start with the early childhood years when we were being shaped and molded by the people and the world around us. Growing up in a lower-middle class family, my inner script was colored by the struggles of the working class. My parents worked hard for the basics that life had to offer, they stuck close to the rules of religion and society that always seem to keep them in a one-step forward two-step back world.

Life and the confines of raising a family was a struggle, filled with confusion and self doubt. I was like a little mirror sharing and reflecting these same values, struggling to change myself to fit in the world of desire and consumption.

It wasn't until I reached the age of 19 that I began to see the light. Although earlier in my youth, I did come across enlightened people while studying martial arts and photography; I really didn't comprehend the wisdom that was being given to me at that time. At the age of 19, away from the conventional form of education and perusing my dream of becoming a professional photographer, I began to see. I began to learn how our minds work, and the world of knowledge opened up to me like an angel from heaven.

If I were to sum up the general principle, it is knowledge and seeing actuality for what it is. In the Taoist concept of being present in the moment, we experience actuality for what it is not what you want or expect it to be. If we rely on our scripts formulated in our childhood, or by influences from past judgments and experiences, actuality eludes us, and we no longer see what is. Life is a continuous flow of changes. Our goal is to see and understand these changes and adapt to them. We do this by expanding our understanding by knowledge and learning. It is the not knowing that creates fear, anger, depression, and the need to control those things that we really cannot control.

I am one of the few that gets to make a living by doing what I truly desire to do. I have had my photography business Fotografata da Duvall Inc. for over 20 years and am blessed to meet a wide verity of people every day.

Beauty Tip: *Make family more than just a word. Take quality time out of each day and each week to spend with family and friends.*

Scott Duvall
fotografatadaduv@qwest.net

36

No More Grey
Beth Minardi

For as long as I can remember, I have always been aware of
the power of color. For Easter, my mom and dad hid eggs in our
yard and I recall being captivated by the intensity of the colors
of the eggs. Even the Easter grass in the basket and the new
spring grass and flowers on the ground were powerful. Color
always intrigued me as a child and little did I know the lasting
impact it would have on my life and my career choice.

I didn't start beauty school until I had been out of college for
almost a year, so I was a bit older than most of the other students. Because of my age, I was chosen to work with many of
the older women who came into the school, primarily for a wash
and set and grey coverage.

At first, I was intimidated by color application, afraid that I
would wreck the color of someone's hair. Once I lost the initial
fear, I began taking great satisfaction in my clients' joy when
their once grey hair was changed to a more natural-looking
shade that took years off their appearance.

The first time I performed a makeover on a client, I
returned a woman's hair to the soft brown she remembered
having when she was a kid. She and I both thought she looked
wonderful – particularly when I brushed through her young-
looking, shiny hair. She and I were both convinced that I had
discovered the fountain of youth.

Since that time, I have perfected the art of coloring hair and
have been very successful in making sure all of my clients are
satisfied with their new look. It still amazes me how my lifelong interest in color has impacted my life as well as the lives
of many others.

Beauty Tip: *Soak your feet in ice cold water for 30 seconds! You'd
be surprised how this energizes the entire body, and makes
you feel super fresh! Buff feet dry with a towel—then jump
into a hot tub and relax for five more minutes. You might*

57

try adding a few drops of Bergamot or Grapefruit essential oils to the tub and just breathe in the wonderful fragrance.

Beth Minardi

38

Matchmaker
Chris Vandehey

The people in the beauty industry are more than technicians, more than entrepreneurs, and even more than artists. For many clients, we are the deepest of friends.

When I began as a licensed hairdresser in Oregon, I worked in a small lease salon trying to make ends meet. This is when I was first blessed with such great clients to grow with. Karen and Reiko, a mother-daughter team, are still with me 26 years later.

Reiko was only 2 years old then and cute as she could be. For some reason there was always this very special connection between us that just became stronger and stronger through out the years.

Her mother, Karen, was a school teacher. I always admired the way she cared for and guided her children. She was never heavy- handed with them and always respected their choices and interests. Her children have all grown into lovely adults.

When Reiko was growing up I loved to have fun with her. And even now, we still get a kick remembering things like "Reiko, did you know that chocolate milk comes from brown cows?"

When she was going through the dating game, I was there to explain to her what was going on. I wanted to be supportive and I wanted her to be happy, for she is beautiful inside and out.

I saw Karen and Reiko every four weeks in the salon and they really became like family. One day we were chatting about Reiko and some of the guys she was dating.

Cliff my business partner suggested that one of his young male clients might be great for her. Well, they agreed to meet and "Bingo!" It was a match! Two years later they are happily married!

How proudly I stood at her wedding while people came to me asking if I was the "hairdresser who got them together." To

39

see her grow into such a lovely, radiant young woman makes me proud and very lucky to be part of their life.

The story I'm sharing is an example of why I absolutely love what I do. It's the human element. That is the true reward. How fulfilling it was for me that Reiko found her soul mate.

Beauty Tip: *When using professional conditioning and styling products, such as Aquage Hair Products, always comb the product through with a comb, not just your hands. This way the product is evenly distributed to give maximum results.*

Chris Vandehey
Owner, "Style on 2nd"
Portland, OR

40

Better Than a Box of Chocolates
Daniel Keane

I had opened an upscale salon in downtown Seattle. I worked about 10 hours a day behind the chair and haunted the local television station offering to do makeovers, demos, anything to get media exposure. My business grew, and I soon had a reputation as one of Seattle's "It" guys in the beauty business.

One day, my wife called the salon, crying and frantic. Our 11- month-old son, Andrew, had burned his hands on the fireplace, and she was heading to the hospital. I followed, and for the next two weeks, we watched the compassionate and loving team in the burn unit caring for our son with kid gloves. I could see that Andrew trusted them. Twice a day he would hold out his little hands, covered with burns, and let the nurses do the painful work of scrubbing away his burned skin. At the end of two weeks, I inherited that job, and I appreciated those nurses even more.

I sent the nurses a box of chocolates, and asked them what I could do to make their tough job easier. They said, "Do something for the long-term care patients." So once a month they set up a room, rolled in full-length mirrors from occupational therapy, and I did hair for the patients.

My first "client" was a 16-year-old girl, a petite brunette with a pretty smile who had learned the hard way not to get into a car with a friend who was drinking. Her neck was broken, so she wore a "halo," a metal brace that encircled her neck and shoulders, with four metal screws that went into the bones in her head. I carefully worked around the device. When I got into my car, I sobbed. What had I gotten myself into? But I kept going back.

At first, I was simply grateful for how the doctor and nurses had helped my son Andrew, and wanted to give something back. There was a big fringe benefit - as I did hair for more patients, I became more grateful. After a day doing hair for up

41

to 20 patients, I would often leave the hospital, cry in my car, and then go home to hug my family. I stopped taking life for granted. I saw how blessed I was and how much I could give. It spilled over into my work at the salon, and I enjoyed my work even more.

I went once a month for seven years, and then one day someone called from the local television station, wanting to do a piece on my "hospital salon." I was surprised to hear from them. I had completely stopped trying to "get my name out there." Apparently, someone at the hospital had noticed that having their hair done, built up the confidence of the long-term patients. This enabled them to be transferred to a convalescent center much more quickly!

I know now that when someone sits down in my chair, they aren't just coming to get their hair done. They're offering me their trust. How I help them feel about themselves is as important as how good I make them look.

Beauty Tip: *Don't deprive yourself of a little choco-late every now and then. We all need to treat our-selves to something. It makes us feel good, and feeling good leads to wonderful self-confidence.*

Daniel Keane
djkeane32@hotmail.com

Follow Your Heart

Rodney R. Rohlfing

When I became a cosmetologist, I dreamed of becoming a platform artist. I felt it would be the ultimate achievement to be on stage teaching the latest trends and techniques to my peers. I started by shampooing hair and getting the models ready for the show. One day, I talked with a man, Jack, who was doing a little of everything to get ready for the show; I had no idea who he was. He asked me about my goals; when I told him I wanted to be a platform artist, I then learned that he was one of the owners of Scruples, a budding new company. I later became one of their artists.

Over the years there have been many transitions in my career, both in the salon and on stage. At a show in Birmingham, Alabama, I saw a lady in the audience who was bald. I thought, "She has more going on than anyone else in the room. She has self-confidence to come to a show like that." Seeing her, bald and without a hairpiece, sitting in the audience and focused on hair made me realize what confidence is all about.

43

I started working with wigs because there was a need in my area. One day I was waiting for a cancer patient when three ladies walked in the door: a little girl, a middle-aged woman, and a senior woman with more hair than she knew what to do with. I thought "please Lord, don't let it be the little girl. I don't think I can do that." Thankfully it was the older lady. She sat down in my chair, and I found a hairpiece I thought would work. She wanted it long so she could put it up. As I was examining her hair to find a color match, she advised me to "be careful." I soon discovered that all of those curls were actually her own hair that had fallen out. Her daughter had been styling her hair at home. When the wig arrived, it was so think and long; she wouldn't let me cut it because of her personal beliefs. She wanted to wear it up like she always wore it. All I could say was "lady, it's not really yours."

At first, I didn't have wigs in my salon to show. I worked with a client to select a wig that would match her natural hair color and enliven her appearance as her cancer treatment progressed. She was nervous about not seeing it and trying it on first. She went to the city to buy one she could see first. One day she called me in desperation for help. When she walked in, I thought the color and cut of her wig looked pretty good. She explained that it was the wig I sold her. She tearfully revealed the wig she bought in the city. I couldn't believe a shop specializing in wigs for cancer patients gave so little thought to how she would look in the wig.

Thank goodness I followed my heart. Giving a cancer patient a realistic look is a great feeling. Most people can't go out without a hairpiece like the lady in the audience. Making someone feel confident when they don't feel beautiful is an awesome achievement. I love giving the gift of confidence.

44

Beauty Tip: *Take care of the hair you've been blessed with. Every other month, add a tablespoon of baking soda to your shampoo to strip your hair of the harsh chemicals we use and come in contact with everyday.*

Rodney R. Rohlfing

Lean Not On Your Own Understanding
Shawn L. Brown

It was October 14, 1998. I was bedridden and seven months pregnant but that was the least of my worries at the time. Our home was in foreclosure, both of our vehicles had been repossessed, and the wedding ring I so deeply cherished was missing. My pride was deteriorating. So I prayed to God that He would just let me die. I believed that I was nothing without my material wealth. What would people think? Even worse what would they say? Approximately 24 hours after my prayer, He answered.

The next evening I was being transferred by a critical care team to a hospital an hour away from home.

My blood pressure was 230 over 120, my kidneys and liver were failing, and we were told that I probably would not live past the weekend.

I did survive the weekend but the months following my hospital visit presented several life threatening challenges. I had two surgeries, a seizure, a blood transfusion, minor heart failure, infections, and delivered a two pound preemie with an infection in his blood stream. Over and over again I cried out, "Why?"

The answer was simple. God had a purpose for my life and it wasn't being fulfilled. He needed me to be humble and seeking before I would be responsive to His calling for my life.

After my illness I decided to pursue a career in the beauty industry, an industry that had always fascinated me. In November 2003 my best friend, my mother, and I opened a salon and I accepted a position as the director of education for a consulting and coaching firm specializing in helping people build successful salons and spas.

My husband and I have two gorgeous children, Quinton, 5 and Lena, 3. We are thankful that God made us realize what is valuable in life. I am now living the life I love, a life filled with purpose, joy and peace. I am confident that God loved me enough to allow me to withstand the greatest test and to become a living, breathing testimony of His grace and mercy. I am a

45

new creation and an eye witness to the power of restoration. So remember, when you are gripped by fear and doubt just, "Trust in the Lord with all your heart and lean not on your own understanding; in all your ways acknowledge him, and he will make your paths straight." Proverbs 3:5-6

Beauty Tip: *To maintain or achieve gorgeous healthy hair, towel dry your hair prior to applying conditioner. Hair that is full of water is unable to absorb anything else. Squeezing your hair is not enough, but towel drying your hair will allow your hair to properly absorb the conditioner leaving you with healthy, shiny hair.*

Shawn L. Brown
shawnbrown@salonepiphany.com
www.salonepiphany.com
www.durocherenterprises.com

46

You Never Know What the Day Will Bring
Vision Chapman

It was just before Christmas, and the salon smelt of pine and cinnamon from the candle burning in the entry. My mom, Gail, and I were in the salon that day; we had a booked schedule. The day was beginning with our first clients of the morning. Gail was getting her client ready for her "holiday do." Her client, a long-time friend of the family, was all set with coffee in hand and eating holiday cookies. Gail was going about her normal "making the client feel special" routine.

I heard them laugh; it was cut short with gurgled sound. From the corner of my eye, I saw Gail jump up saying, "Oh, my gosh! Call 911!" I knew it was serious. I recalled saying to myself, "Okay this is when you want to remain the 3 Cs. 'calm, cool, collected'." I leaned down and put my ear next to Gail's client, and noticed she wasn't able to breathe and turning very pale. So, I tapped into my mind – to 10 years ago – the Heimlich maneuver and CPR, which I had learned at the Toni & Guy Academy. It was now or never. If I didn't do something by the time the paramedics arrived, it would be too late; I reached down with both hands just below her rib cage but above the stomach and with one great heave lifted the client and chair off the ground! A deflating sound was heard, like that of a balloon, and the cookie hit the mirror with a sound that I will remember for all time. The room gave a sigh of relief as we all just stood around the room in silence trying to fathom what just happened. About 10 minutes later the paramedics arrived, and it wasn't until one of them shook my hand and said, "good job," that I realized the gravity of what had happened. What if things would have turned out differently? Our lives would be changed forever.

We never know as image creators what the day will bring in the salon environment – what challenges will turn up or what we will have to overcome. After all, we work with a very important material – people and their feelings. We have the potential

47

In Beauty

to change lives with the snips we make or the colors we choose. One of the most important things in being an image creator or beauty maker is education. Just as in this story, we never know when we will have to pull from past experiences. We might not know what the day will bring to the salon, but that makes what we do exciting and rewarding. It is important for us to stay current and to inspire our clients to do the same. After all, we are dealing with the creation of something they wear everyday – their image.

Beauty Tip: *Let the stress out! Create something – whether you color, play with clay, sew something, etc. Just go out and create. It takes your mind off your problems and lets you focus on you.*

Vision Chapman
christian@seattlemodel.com
noboundaries3@aol.com

Living with Purpose
Dr. David Nickel

"My hair was falling out. I had the classic male pattern baldness syndrome. I was 33 and in a panic…Less than one year on Live Vitamins and all my hair has returned," reported J. H. from California.

C. P., a 31-year old female from Oregon, excitedly told me on the phone what happened in less than 3 months after taking Live Vitamins. "My skin cleared up; I had more energy, and I slept better. I no longer get the shakes, and the dark circles under my eyes are gone."

These and many other healthy happy stories continue to inspire me. The PrimeZyme Vision focuses on people living in health, vitality and beauty, and the PrimeZyme Mission is to provide everyone Live Vitamins for vital health and beauty.

At the age of 2, I was in a full body cast for seven months and then on foot braces for two months. I had a severe bone infection called osteomyelitis and was not expected to live.

The daily prayers of my mother and father and the support of doctors, friends and the church resulted in my mother always referring to me as God's miracle boy. By the age of 15, I clearly knew my purpose in life and that was to serve others. For me, there is no greater satisfaction than making a difference in someone's life.

I had enjoyed serving others in many different professions until the age of 38. It was then that I found my prime focus: Natural Chinese Medicine. My true purpose was to assist Mother Nature in supporting the healing of others. My dream was to follow in the footsteps of my hero, one of the greatest doctors of all time, Sun Si Miao. He wrote in his book the first major chapter in Chinese medicine on diet therapy, 600 years after the birth of Jesus. He said "…those applying diet for treatment are superb physicians. Diet therapy is recommended first."

I enjoy nothing more than being the Santa Clause of Mother Nature. Now, I can share my ultimate gift: the rediscovered

49

medical evidence and the safe Live Vitamin Enzyme Foods that work for beauty. These prime vegetable and protein foods support waking up the beauty and the life you love in beauty every day. What Hippocrates (the father of Western medicine) said, over 2,000 years ago, is just as true then as now: "Let thy food be thy medicine and thy medicine be thy food."

You are invited now to visit your Live Vitamin Food Store at primezyme.com and explore what beauty kit(s) may be right for you.

Beauty Tip: *To look, and feel better I recommend the following:*
  For the beginner, EZ Skin Kit I
  For advanced the EZ Pro Beauty Kit III
  These products are available at the Live
  Vitamin Store: www.primezyme.com

Dr. David J. Nickel
www.primezyme.com

50

A Day Like Today
Nancy Ferguson

It must be time for the alarm to sound by now. In the past, there have been choices made and steps taken to prepare for today. The house is alive with enthusiasm.

Anxious to slip into those fresh new socks and secure that shiny new belt buckle to complete this image. Finally it's time to leave the house. As the door closes, a sense of confidence radiates out into the crisp morning air. The roar of the engine marks a turning point as the car pulls out. The vehicle seems to be familiar with this path yet there is a newness to this journey. As the car slows to a stop at our destination, the doors swing wide open to the possibilities that await. From this point, we are seconds away from joining the crowd. The faces in the throng display curiosity, excitement, and uncertainty.

Whatever this day holds we know what it took to get here and that things will be different at this time next year.

Therefore I won't be a partial participant in this moment. I made my first appointment late this morning so that I could be here completely, to walk through the halls with my son as he enters the first day of the last year of grade school.

I returned to my car where I sat in silence for a while. I thought about how things are always moving forward, regardless of the pace. I replayed in my mind the look on the faces of the kindergarten children as they embarked on what would be the foundation for their future. I thought about how they would aspire to be a fifth grader like my son, with all of the style and confidence. Granted, at grade five they are not ready to run a business or the country, but they don't appear to be afraid to try.

At that point I decided to approach my day as if it were the first day of fifth grade.

I strutted into every transaction with style, confidence. At the end of the day, the results more than doubled my expectation and I couldn't wait for the next day.

51

WAKE UP...LIVE THE LIFE YOU LOVE

I realized that inspiration can be in any shape or size when you are open to seeing it! Each of us can approach everyday with the same spirit and emotion of youth and assurance. Each of us can make that decision. Everyone should experience a day like today.

Beauty Tip: Beauty comes from within. If you take care of that first, then anything you do on the outside will be amplified.

Nancy Ferguson

52

Friends

Dwight Cox

There are a number of people who will tell you that their relationship with a beautymaker changed their lives. Many of us in the beauty business are proud of the influence we have in the lives of our friends – our clients. I know that's true, because I have been on both sides of the equation.

I was working in a manufacturing plant and going to school at the University of Northern Alabama. I hated my job: depressing, regular, offering no variety and no sense of humanity. Unexpectedly, something interesting happened. I answered an ad for a "hair model."

The hair artist on the platform was Rodney Rohlfing. He has such a zest for life; such a passion for his craft, that I was electrified. I saw that beautymaking was creative, artistic, expressive and had a powerful effect on people. I wanted to do that.

Melissa, my wife, encouraged me to go to school to learn hair. Through her sacrifice, I did it.

What I found was a profession filled with everything I had been missing: people, constant change, challenge, excitement and meaning. My new job was not so much a means to a paycheck as it was a way of life.

Then, in September of 2002, I went to learn about Bio-ionics, a new treatment for hair. While at the workshop, I met another beautymaker who had come to study, as well. He looked familiar, but I couldn't place him. Then, when I heard his voice, the penny dropped: it was Rodney Rohlfing.

When we met again it was as fellow professionals instead of artist and model. We have become good friends, and I am now a platform artist in training. He has really helped me grow professionally.

Many really wonderful doors have opened because of those two meetings with Rodney, and I hope I am a good reflection of his example. Sometimes, I see things that encourage me to believe that I am.

One such case was a personal trainer who was a bit of a celebrity in our community. She was a real success story as a single mom with three children who made a good home. But all her over-processed hair told me that she had low self-esteem. Her posture and eye-contact said the same.

After we cut, colored and treated her hair, her attitude changed. We saw the woman she was and brought it out. Now, she is truly dynamic. She "works a room" because now, she sees what I saw: she sees beauty.

I don't believe there is such a thing as an ugly woman, but there are some uninformed women. We can always do something for her.

And we're always ready to do it.

Beauty Tip: *Don't destroy your hair or your beauty with over processing. Listen to your stylist, and find a look and a style that comes from your personality and suits your lifestyle. Be sensible, and keep your hair healthy – nothing looks better.*

Dwight Cox

54

A Letter of Love and Gratitude
Cherisse White

Editor's Note: Beautymakers learn that true beauty comes from within and it comes when you least expect it. True beauty touches and changes lives. The White family reminds us powerfully of this truth.

Dearest Montana Lafayette,

An angel was born to Cherisse and Chuck White on April 28, 1998. She was called Montana Lafayette White. This angel brought three miracles. The first miracle was your quick birth. Daddy held you, changed your diaper on his very own, sang to you and kept saying "Montana." By early that morning, you were responding to your given name. I held you close to my chest, hummed to you and called you mama's "lil pooh." We both experienced so much comfort. Two days later at home while breastfeeding, you just quit breathing with no clear answer as to why.

Our second miracle came when you persevered another week in the hospital. We had such incredible love and support from everyone. People across the world were praying for you. We had buttons made of your beautiful face and gave them to everyone that visited you. Everyone asked about that "beautiful baby!" We replied with "that's our angel – Montana, a gift from God." You quietly passed away May 8, 1998. The doctors said it was from Sudden Infant Death Syndrome.

The third miracle is your gift of pure love and good magic. We know you chose us as your parents and for that, we are proud.

During your short time with us, we fell in love with you. You impacted and blessed our lives. You brought great joy and a greater understanding of the meaning of family and friends. You came and opened us – now there's so much more to see. You are the most beautiful baby! Our lives have changed; we have a stronger relationship with each and other and with God. We are truly better parents, and people who know us or have heard

55

our story have become better parents. Thank you for blessing us with our own Guardian Angel.

You will always be in our hearts,

Mommy and Daddy

Montana's beautiful memory is still making a difference. Our dream is to make it a safer place for babies to come into this world. More than $30,000.00 has been given in the name of Montana Lafayette White to help grieving families and some day find an answer to SIDS. Some of those charities include Northern California SIDS Alliance and Helping After Neonatal Death of Santa Clara.

Beauty Tip: Enjoy life right now because it is a gift! Consider journaling because, it keeps you in touch with your life and lets all of your feelings and thoughts out. You have a choice of how you respond to the roller coaster of life. Be true to your emotions because it might be the last time you get to!

Cherisse White
www.cherisseshairsalon.com

Success: Taking It Personally

Jack R. Sanders

There is a difference between personal and professional success, yet they have a synergy with each other. The first thought that most people have when asked about success is a dollar amount. I've realized over the years that financial success is secondary to the feeling of success in my heart each day. When one obtains happiness and success in their professional life, their personal life improves as well. The following are a few key questions you must ask yourself to obtain professional success.

Is your outlook good? To keep growing and increasing your business in this industry, you must maintain a positive attitude. Our salon team knows the importance of this philosophy.

We know that our mood has to be in sync so we can create and radiate the attitude and culture we have at our salon, Technical Artistry.

Are you excited to go to work and be the best you can be? Treat each day like it's your last! Excitement is contagious and it will spread to your clients and throughout your environment when you love your job.

Do your loved ones encourage you? When my wife Kris tells me to "knock their socks off," I know she truly believes I can. Her confidence in my ability inspires me to feel the same about myself. When a client senses my confidence, they know they've come to the right place!

Do you let your personal problems upset your professional well being?

For eight months I worked at a salon and not even my coworkers knew I was getting a divorce. Why? Because I was committed to making my client's experience the best it could be.

Do you treat every experience as a learning experience? Always look at the positive and ask yourself what you have learned. Doing so will help you down the road. Believe me, there will always be a "next time".

57

In Beauty

At the end of each day, do you feel satisfied that you have performed at the highest level of which you are capable? I do. I go home each day with the satisfaction of knowing that I have touched someone's life. Often the attention, concern, and finesse with which you treat a salon guest is more important to them than you could possibly imagine.

Take pride in your work and extract happiness from each day!

Beauty Tip: *One of the key points of working with a guest in the salon is explaining to them how to re-create their look at home. It's important that the hair is 75-80% dry before you start working with your tools. When you start using your tools, be sure the blow dryer is directed down the hair shaft. Working from the head shape out to the ends will keep the hair from looking fuzzy. To add volume, be sure and lift the hair above its natural falling position and by working down the hair shaft, you'll add to the final look of healthy, shinny, beautiful hair.*

Jack R. Sanders
jack@techartsalon.com
www.techartsalon.com

58

Just to Say Thank You
Jack Leighan

A few years ago, I was relocating my salon. After opening one day, a client I had not seen in 10 years walked through the door and presented me with a plant as a welcome to the neighborhood gift. I welcomed Peter with a hug; he gave me the plant and told me that his home was just up the street. He wanted to make an appointment because he said he had a story to tell me. We went to the appointment book, and I found a suitable time for us to get together.

Peter's appointment was the first one of the day; so, after we were settled on our haircut task, he started his story. Peter told me how when I cut his hair it made him feel more confident and self-assured. Peter is an intelligent college professor, but I had given him the confidence he needed to approach this beautiful woman at his favorite bookstore. A couple of years later, he married this woman, and now, they had two beautiful children. He wanted to tell me thank you for giving him the life that he lives every day.

Peter said most of the time in life when someone touches you in a positive way we never say thank you! So he wanted to thank me in person. As you can imagine I was floored, happy, excited, honored; I mean what do you say to that?

We went into a deep philosophical discussion about after what happens when we pass on. If, during our funeral, we could sit and watch all the people that we touched in a special way all lined up single file, how we would of course recognize our immediate family members and close friends, but the majority of people we would not recognize at all. For most of them, we might say, "I have never met that person," or "Am I at the right funeral?" But somewhere, sometime, we had a positive affect on that person and possibly changed their life in a powerful way. Hair designers do these tasks every day!

59

Beauty Tip: *If you straighten your hair, you should use a small amount of Kpak Smoothing Balm from Joico. Use this on the front of your hair then a small amount for the back half, using a comb to get the product distributed evenly which will give you a much better end result. Then, use a Mason Pearson brush, and your hair will be fantastic.*

Jack Leighan
hellogorgeous@dsl-only.net

60

Try Something New
Helene Picard

Beauty isn't just a look, haircut, or attitude. It is something intangible that comes from within. The key to success for hair connoisseurs is giving the most beautiful experience an individual can enjoy.

We find the most beautiful things are perceived to have an inner glow which is visible on the outside too. It is no different in people. This glow is actually confidence in each of us. To be beautiful, you must nurture and love yourself inside and out; physically, mentally and spiritually to be beautiful. It doesn't matter if you are a parent, spouse or friend; being good to yourself will make you better for those you love.

"Putting beauty into our bodies to get beauty out of our bodies" is my focus when working with clients. It can be something as simple as a new haircut or color; radiant skin after a facial, an aromatherapeutic massage, or an eye-catching manicure and pedicure.

Allow yourself to be known and understood by your salon and spa technician or other beauty creator. During consultation, offer as much information as possible about yourself and your lifestyle. We know, as professionals, that nobody has enough time in the morning to prepare themselves for that "million-dollar" look. We all have images of what we think we "should" look like and therefore, we are often disappointed with the outcome, especially when it hasn't met our "vision."

Share that vision with us and we can help you. Think outside the box! If a big change is uncomfortable, start small. But start, nonetheless, and then continue with the suggested changes. It starts with trust. Trust your beauty creator to help you reveal the true beauty within. Trust someone to shampoo your hair. Trust their styling creativity. Trust us to bring out the love you have for yourself for all to see. Beauty is perception; the better you feel about yourself, the better you will be perceived.

61

Think about how you feel when you leave a salon with a terrific haircut. You feel ready to conquer the world. This confidence can make a world of difference in your daily life.

So go for it! Make some changes, whether subtle or extreme. You'll be amazed at how you feel and how you look.

Beauty Tip: *Tell your Beautymaker what you really want and don't be afraid to recount horror stories from the past. Be honest!*

Helene Picard
www.hairconnoisseurs.com
helene@hairconnoisseurs.com

62

In Beauty

Living Life On Your Own Terms
Jamea Garlinger

Paula worked just up the street at a state office in Sacramento. One day, she had the afternoon off and decided to come to the salon for a new shampoo. I helped her to select one and gave her a tour of our salon. I also cut her hair, which marked the beginning of our friendship.

She told me she was divorced, a mother of three, and new to this area. She had short, thick, spiked hair so I took a few minutes to formulate a unique hair style for her. She loved her new look and I loved this new friendship.

I always looked forward to seeing Paula. She would share her experiences and because of her stories and insight, I turned to her as a mentor. Only in her forties, Paula had been through so much and had even gone through surgery and chemo treatments for breast cancer but was happy to reveal that the cancer was in remission. After hearing about this, I made it my goal to make her feel as special as possible.

At one appointment, she had mentioned that her cancer had returned. Now it was in her spinal cord. She had decided to undergo radiation once again to fight the cancer that was plaguing her body.

On Paula's treatment day, she would stop by the salon on her way back from the hospital. Sometimes she would get her hair done, other times she just wanted to hold my infant daughter for comfort therapy. Paula found much happiness in holding and rocking my daughter.

She kept up this routine for an entire year until my second daughter was born. She loved the girls and I loved and trusted her. Paula became family to us. She would often come by the house on Saturdays just to see the girls, a visit which brought her much comfort and joy.

The cancer forced Paula to retire, so she decided to move to be with her family. One day, I received a call from the hospital.

It was Paula. The radiation treatments were not working as she had hoped. Without hesitation, I took three days off from work, packed up the kids, and headed to the hospital. We visited for hours, we hugged and we cried. I knew it was the last time I would see her. A short time later, Paula's fight against cancer was over. Paula taught me to live my life to the fullest regardless of what others think. She taught me to listen to my heart, to safeguard my vision, ambition, and drive. Paula lived her life on her own terms and taught me to do the same.

I have been a stylist for 23 years and a salon owner for the past 15. I stay in the business because it feels wonderful to make people feel great about themselves. There is no other business that has this level of kindness, flexibility, and closeness to our clients. As a beauty professional we have the power to make a difference in our clients' lives.

Beauty Tip: *Buy a full length mirror for yourself. Before you go out the door in the morning assess yourself from head to toe. Do you like what you see? Do your shoes need polish? Do your clothes match? Do you look like someone who is successful in life? This is a great tool. Use it daily and, "Look your best everyday."*

Jamea Garlinger
jamea@sbcglobal.net

Open for Business
Regina Webb

"You can't swim out into the ocean until you leave the shore." I repeated this quote to myself as I turned in my resignation. With my resignation in, I was on my way to opening Regina Webb Salon & Spa in Bowling Green, Kentucky.

Since I was four years old, playing with hair in my mother's salon, I knew I wanted to make a difference. I started and completed beauty college before I graduated high school. Within six month of my high school graduation, I purchased my own salon.

After a short time, my husband was drafted into the Army, and I gave up my salon to move with him. It was then that I began a career with the Mercantile Corporation and was honored as the Mercantile Top Producer of the Year for five-consecutive years, producing over $300,000 annually from hairstyling services and retail sales.

A membership with The Salon Association changed the course of my career. I absorbed everything the association taught about opening a salon and spa "the right way." I was excited to put these ideas into practice by starting my own business again, but I was nervous about the risk. My pastor inspired me to follow my dreams not matter what the cost might be. I was deeply moved when he asked me, "Do you want people to remember you for how much money you have or for how many lives you have touched?"

In 1999, I opened the Regina Webb Salon & Spa. In the second year of business, the salon grew 150 percent and was name one the "Top 200 Fastest Growing Salons" by *Salon Today Magazine*. By Christmas 2001, we had outgrown our original salon location and moved into our new 7,800 square foot European-style facility. The Bowling Green Daily News named me the "Best of the Best Hairstylist" and my salon the "Best of the Best Salon and Spa." I also became an Intercolffure Mondlal North America member, a Redken performing artist, a Redken

ambassador salon, a Salon City Press Club Mag Artist and
have been appointed by the governor as a board member of the
Kentucky State Board of Cosmetology.

The balance between technical skills and business skills has
been the key to my professional success. My main concern is
that many hairstylists open their own salon or spa because of
their superior technical skills, yet lack the business education
or skills necessary to own and manage a business. My personal
vision as a leader in the professional beauty industry is to raise
the educational level of cosmetologists in order to elevate the
prestige of our profession.

After 30 years in the professional beauty industry, I have
learned that the foundation of this business is to make another
person feel good, whether the person is a client or an employee.
In fact, I believe that it is the foundation of success in life.

Regina Webb
Bowling Green, Kentucky

66

Healing Beyond Belief

Annemarie Camenzind

In May of 2000, a mammogram indicated and a biopsy confirmed one of a woman's biggest fears – breast cancer. The doctors advised me to immediately undergo a mastectomy. In my desperation, I recalled an incident that happened several months earlier.

While shopping, a former client of mine came up to me and told me how she used a Native American cream made of powerful herbs to heal herself of a melanoma. She showed me the small faint scar in place of the lesion. She felt I needed to know this as a skin-care educator. Impressed with her claim, I filed this experience.

I grew up in Switzerland, where holistic medicine and organic food are used more commonly than here in the U.S. I had always taken good care of myself and had an interest in natural healing, nutrition and herbal therapy. Like Hippocrates I believed that given the right conditions, the body heals itself. I believed his statement, "Let thy food be your medicine and let thy medicine be your food."

Overwhelmed by my shocking diagnosis, I received the news that the financing for my new school building had come through. Life was going to provide me with what I needed. On that day, I decided not to follow the doctor's advice and to take my healing into my own hands. I ordered the healing cream.

A guardian angel was guiding me along the way. Helpful people entered my life, as I needed them. A retired doctor with a reputation for his holistic treatment became my coach. True to his reputation, the doctor felt that cancer is the outcome of underlying causes that must be addressed and healed. He was also familiar with the Native American herbal cream. He diagnosed me with several problems: weak liver and adrenals, environmental toxins, difficulty in absorbing protein, parasites and nutritional deficiencies. It was an impressive list compared to the allopathic test results that showed my body to be in good health!

The herbal cream arrived and proved to be a black cream based on bloodroot.

With one application being sufficient, I applied the tiniest amount on the biopsy scab.

67

Immediately, a searing pain shot into my breast and traveled to my armpit. It lasted all night. I was hot and drank 12 glasses of water. I guessed this was the healing process.

The next morning I knew that the cancer had gone. My next job was to build immunity and attend to the underlying problems.

One week after the application of the cream, my doctor had me do the AMAS blood test for cancer detection. The results were negative.

As part of my treatment, I had my mercury fillings removed and went through a detoxification program. As I continued my immune-building routine, I put myself on a low-fat cleansing/healing diet including fresh fruit and vegetable juice, 90 percent raw food, herbs and supplements and specific foods to create alkalinity in the body while adding yoga and Kneipp therapy (hot and cold therapy). I also applied frankincense daily on my breasts and used several recommended naturopathic electrical devices for healing. Regular massage and aromatherapy were also part of my routine.

Throughout the following weeks, my focus was to heal myself. I only told those close to me about my health condition. I never used the "c" word, as I did not want to affirm its presence in my life. Friends who urged me to take the typical course of action were asked to stay away. Truthfully, I must admit I have lost some along the way. Two months after the diagnosis, a thermogram revealed that my breast was "clean."

This challenge became a peak experience in my life – first, because of the way it unfolded, and secondly, because my beliefs ultimately healed me. It cemented my knowledge that my purpose in life is teaching and healing. What I teach is not just theory it works. It is possible for everyone to take control of their healing and do the same.

Beauty Tip: *A diet of organic, raw food rejuvenates the body and helps to prevent diseases, such as cancer. This would include food combining and emphasizing foods that promote an alkaline system.*

Annemarie Camenzind

You Never Know

Eric Fisher

Sometimes in life we come across someone that makes us realize what we truly do for a living.

One day a woman in her early 20's from a small Kansas town, Jerry Sue, came into the salon. Accompanying her was her big bundles of hair.

Jerry Sue was very nervous. She began shaking when we started the interview process – she had never been to a salon.

She had saved her money for a year just to come to the salon. She said that it was one of the biggest things in her life. When I started to study her face during the consultation, I could see that she was a beautiful girl.

Jerry had an engaging smile, beautiful sparkling eyes and a sense of presence, but all anyone could see was that she was hiding behind a bad hairstyle, no makeup, a sweat shirt and a pair of jeans.

She said, "Make me look my best; do whatever you want to do." Our salon's slogan is "Authentic Beauty." We want to understand the individual client and make it an individual approach.

I got more excited as I cut her hair and exposed her face. She started to smile.

Her hair was monochromatic; she needed color but had no more money. We did color for nothing. We then went above and beyond. We waxed her brows and continued with "natural looking" makeup.

I walked over as they were blowing her hair, and I couldn't believe it. It made me stumble with my words. She started crying really loud.

I said to her, "Save your money; go to the Gap, and buy a black dress to show off your shape." Before she left, I gave her hair products to take with her. She gave me hugs and kisses.

Two weeks later, she came into the salon wearing a little black dress. She brought homemade cookies and a card. Jerry Sue looked me straight into my eyes and said, "I don't know how to thank you. My personality has changed. I have come out of my shell."

It really changed her life. It reinforced that we can create a life changing experience for someone.

Beauty Tip: *The more you give, the more you get. Everything isn't measured by money. It doesn't get any better than this.*

Eric Fisher
ericfishersalon@cox.net

70

The Brand New You
Tamara Aruj

Growing up, I was always told I had an "old soul." This thrilled me. Like all children, nothing seemed better to me than being a grown-up. And I was very pleased, since the childhood-me gave the term "old" a sophisticated gloss. Being called an old soul made me feel wonderfully wise, and I willingly lived up to the persona.

But as an adult, the concept of being an old soul lost its lovely patina. I regretted having had an old-soul-hood rather than a childhood. It would have been far better to have adventured from infancy to teens, growing up without any thought to age or wisdom; to be spontaneous, to be childlike. As an adult, I came to appreciate that while age is inevitable, wisdom is not an inevitable but is a by-product of age.

My daughter helped me to transform these regrets into an inspiring, healthy way to live.

When she was born, I marveled at her newness and naturalness. And I saw that she too was an old soul, but not as I had understood it as a child. She had the uncanny ability and wisdom to grow and change naturally, and appropriately. She learned to crawl, then to balance on her two feet, and then to walk. She handled every new stage with exquisite, happy-go-lucky grace.

And she was always ready to be new again.

By loving her, I grew to love myself more. I saw that I could be new again, as long as I was ready. I also saw that being new had nothing to do with rejecting who I had been yesterday.

She showed me that becoming a new person means participating in how the world is meant to work. Newborns, new moons, new years – all are part of our lives. And they change, without ever losing their essential selves.

Being renewed means knowing that it is safe and worthwhile to make changes and to honor the effortless person often hidden inside our effortful, and unchanging, outside selves.

When we are ready to be new again, the world reveals itself to us as an enormous opportunity for learning. The childlike adult I have become understands far more than the old-soul child I grew up as, ever did.

Beauty Tip: *Breathe! Nourish your body, mind and soul by breathing deeply at least 5 minutes a day and whenever possible throughout the day. Breathing deeply brings more revitalizing energy into our bodies, directly benefiting our physical and mental well-being and the quality of our lives. "Life is in the breath; therefore he who only half breathes, half lives." –Yogic Proverb*

Tamara Aruj
www.thebrandnewyou.com

72

Jose's Story

Jose Figueroa

There is a fine line between victory and defeat—a subtle shift in mindset and the ability to ride out the storms. I'll admit it's not always easy, especially when you're down in the dumps or out in the streets.

Looking back on my life, I realize how different it has become. If I had given up, I would not have the success I have today. Everything in my life—my friends, my business, and people I have encouraged—would not be here had I given up. To give up can be called a tragedy.

Los Angeles was my home until I was 16. My mother moved us to live in Mexico when I became involved in alcohol and drugs. At 20, I had cleaned up my act and returned to California to pursue my dream of doing hair.

After I got my license, I had to start my career somewhere. I was giving $8 haircuts in a low-income area of Costa Mesa. I soon built up a following and, my confidence. I was ready for Newport Beach, and before I knew it, I landed a job at a nice salon. Everything seemed great, but it wasn't. I was about to pay my dues.

The salon closed because the owner didn't pay the rent. Nobody in the neighborhood would hire me without clientele. To make matters worse, I ended a three-year live-in relationship. I was homeless and without a job. Now, feeling hopeless, I had myself to depend on. The next six months would prove to be the hardest time of my life. I was involved in four car accidents, lived in my car, and cleaned up at gas stations. Feeling depressed, thoughts of suicide became my constant companion, but somehow I didn't give in.

After six months, I was sick of struggling. I saw a lovely upscale salon, Emerald Salon, and summoned all my courage to ask for a job. Donald Anderson, the owner, saw something in me—what it was I don't know because I looked like a bum and had no self-esteem. He agreed to give me one and only one

73

chance. I am proud to say that not only was I a part of Emerald for four years, but I was also his busiest hairdresser.

I soon met my mentor and coach, Lauren Gartland. I was working on a new set of problems; I wanted to increase my income while working fewer hours! Through Lauren's coaching, I was able to make $100,000 a year working four days a week. Lauren was my guardian angel, friend, and sometimes challenger, but she was always there for me to handout inspiration and guidance.

My next step was obvious—to own my own salon. I had fallen in love with a little seaside community in San Diego called La Jolla. This is where I wanted to be. Once again, I was starting from scratch. Lauren was there to help me design my transition. I opened Salon Jose four years ago. Salon Jose is an intimate six-chair salon with a unique atmosphere.

Everyday I go to work to play. I get paid to have fun and be creative with the Pacific Ocean breezes blowing through my salon. What more could I ask for? Over the years, I have had the privilege of educating all over the country for many great companies like L'Oreal, Tigi, Joico, Bumble and Bumble, and Pytologie.

If you are experiencing hard times, don't give up. That's the most valuable thing you can learn from me. Trust me, things will get better. Just keep moving forward. Once you've tasted a little success, don't rest. Always keep learning – from your colleagues, your competitors, and especially your clients. They always teach me the most. When the going gets tough, don't be afraid to ask for help.

Beauty Tip: *Wait 3 days after any hair color service to wash your hair. If you wash your hair right away, you will wash out 10% of your color the first day, 20% the second day, and 30% the third day. If you wait for your hair to recover for three days, you will only lose 5%.*

Jose Figueroa
jose@salonjose.com
www.salonjose.com

74

Wake Up and Live
Brenda Hunt

I am not qualified by my profession, or my level of education, to give any particular advice in how to succeed in this world other than being true to yourself and your dreams and by sharing those dreams with others. To not only live my life with what I know in my mind but to live with my true heart.

When I opened my salon 22 years ago, my goal, as a stylist, was to exceed my clients' expectations each and every visit. Seeing the smile in my clients' eyes and knowing that they trusted my talents and friendship for so many years was the most gratifying feeling I could imagine. Offering them superior technical service and a place where they could feel connected was a blessing to me.

As the years went by and the staff grew with the demand of business, my goal evolved into not only creating the perfect environment for our clients, but developing a staff of professionals and helping them achieve their goals.

Whether they began at my salon as a student – through training and positive support I watched them grow into the stylists they are today, or they transferred to our salon in search of the perfect environment for them to grow as a professional reaching their own personal and economic levels of success, the joy was there. That is not to say that it always ran smoothly, but I learned quickly to love the journey whatever it may be — never forgetting my purpose. Being able to create an environment where such a fine assemblage of professionals can come together has been my true professional success.

During these years, my husband and I have also been raising two wonderful children, our son Shawn, 19, and our daughter Danielle, 15. Even greater joys have been celebrated in their successes. Just last year when we sent our son away to college in Boston, I sat down one evening and wrote a poem to him.

"I reminded him that life was like an apple, plentiful, radiant and luscious and on occasion, you will find one with a bruise...maybe even a worm (life's challenges) and you will have to decide on what to do with that wonderful apple you have so desired.

The choice is to eat around the bad spot...even spit it out, but not to let that stop you from enjoying your apple."

Beauty Tip: *Life is for the taking. Regardless of the challenges you face, embrace them, for they will make you stronger. Remember that you cannot achieve and value true success without risking failure. Be generous without expectation.*

Brenda Hunt
Salon Owner/Administrative Director
Panache Hair Salon and Day Spa
Whitehouse Station, NJ 08889
908-534-1512 (office)
brenda@panachespa.com
www.panachespa.com

A Life Journey
Gary Gerard

I've spent my adult years sharing and enjoying the cosmetology industry as a salon owner for 17 years while teaching for 23 years at my school. I travel to speak and teach around the world, conducting hair shows. In more than 2,500 educational programs, I have shared my love for the industry while, I hope, motivating and inspiring hairdressers to become their very best.

Can it get any better? Yes, with the help of the most wonderful lifetime friends from all walks of life. The journey has been great and still is. My advice, however humble it may be is this: Whatever career you choose, give it all you've got and enjoy every minute of it. Don't step on anyone while climbing the ladder of success and you will find it to be a much shorter climb than you imagined. Don't look for the end of the journey, for that will only be enjoyed for a minute. The journey will last your lifetime, so spend it well.

Time is really all we have, and not even a minute of it is guaranteed. Life will give back much more than you will ever give it. If you are ever lucky enough to be able to help someone by sharing your wisdom, knowledge or understanding, please do so.

And may your life's journey be full of good karma. Over the years, I have been gratified to receive some awards and recognitions. Imagine what a thrill it was to be inducted into "The Hairdressers Hall of Fame" and to have received the "Lifetime Achievement Award!"

Although I am very proud of my accomplishments, my most prized "trophy" is the warmth and kindness my colleagues and co-workers have shared with me throughout the years. And, as you read this book, I thank you for letting me share a part of my journey with you.

Beauty Tip: *If you promise to always be kind to your hairdresser or barber, I'll share the best kept secret in our industry. Hair* dryers can be very damaging to hair but certain ionic hair-dryers are not. Trust your friend to be a true professional.

Gary Gerard, President
gerards@earthlink.net
www.GaryGerard.com

78

"Wake Up . . . Live the Life You Love"
Evarista Ponce

"As human beings, our greatness lies not so much in being able to remake the world…As in being able to remake ourselves."–Mahatma Gandhi

When I read this quote, I always take a moment and breathe as I allow each word to resonate through my whole being. This has been my mantra for my life this past year.

At the age of 20, I found myself in the depths of the "city that never sleeps," New York. I went to New York on a whim. I never thought I would meet my future husband. One of my dear friends introduced me to this gorgeous man with the most mesmerizing blue eyes. I remember so clearly, sitting at a fountain in mid-town and talking about life till the sun came up. I knew this man was special – different. We were inseparable from that moment on.

I married this young ambitious man, and since both of us were in the business, we decided to settle down in Los Angeles. I had been a make-up artist and stylist in the Bay Area for five years. I had a natural talent for remaking a person from head to toe. My husband was a former model, and photography was a hobby for him. We soon found ourselves with a thriving business. He was the photographer, and I was the creative producer/stylist. We had the perfect life together – at work and at home. Our careers took us all over the world – shooting for *TV Guide*, *Teen Magazine*, *Soap Opera Digest*, Warner Brothers, NBC, UPN, Kenneth Cole, and Academy Award winning actors.

I found my niche' in the Latin market – styling for Ricky Martin and Oscar De La Hoya in commercials. I loved the travel, the creativity, and most of all transforming people and bringing out their best.

One day my whole world came to a standstill. My perfect little life was over. In one moment, "our" life was no more. For the first six months, I questioned why my husband would want to leave me. Was I not pretty enough for him? Not sexy enough?

79

Most of my self-doubt was focused on the external. Focusing on the surface, I failed to look what was going on inside me. Sadness was my daily companion. I was still working with my ex; so I had to keep my composure on the job. I continued transforming people's lives – not knowing my smile was only a façade.

One night as I sat on my sundeck looking up at the stars, I had this realization that I would be all right. I closed my eyes and for the first time in a year, I began to breathe again. I was so lucky to be alive and began to walk with a new confidence and a sort of an inner knowing that didn't exist in me before. My perception soon started to change! I realized my power as a woman and for the first time in a long time, I owned it. I saw life as an opportunity. I create everything. And because of this, I am so engaged in life and my career as a producer has taken off. I continue to transform people's lives daily. Now, I start with what's on the person's inside. It's called alchemy, turning precious metal into gold.

To celebrate my 33rd birthday, I went skydiving – 13,000' out of an airplane. It was amazing. What a journey this year has been. Thanks to those who inspired me and touched my life. And thanks to my ex-husband, I would still be a caterpillar struggling in my cocoon but you have given me my wings to fly.

Beauty Tip: *Yoga is the union of the body and spirit. Your breath, which will bring you back home to yourself time and again. Your breath can be one of the greatest friends or lovers we will ever know.*

Evarista Ponce
evarista@earthlink.net

A Day in the Life of a Death

Margo Blue

I have always lived my life as though "the glass was half full", a term one hears when giving or receiving great advice,...but there are some things, I have discovered, that do not qualify for the option of "full" or "empty."

Take, for instance, PTA meetings: they always occur on an evening when I am exhausted from work, and they are always early in the evening, but end late! Also, baby showers should be a happy occasion: definitely a "no-brainer" on the "must go without a doubt list" like one of my staffs' weddings or the funeral of someone's parent. Now, there is an occasion for which I am never late, unusual for a person like me, as I am always rushing to get to the next point, without the benefit of even going to the bathroom!

Back to a funeral.

Recently, my best friend and mentor, Edwin Neill passed away. When I received the news, I had the same reaction as everyone else. Edwin was our Aveda distributor – a loving, attentive father and husband and an elder full of vision, who taught me the true meaning of integrity. I was always honest and empathetic, but no one could make you feel the impact of your actions, or lack of them, like Edwin. In addition to his title as leader, Edwin ran software, salon and spa equipment companies, and developed, with his talented wife and staff, a seasonal educational getaway: Quality College. My only collegiate experience was going through Edwin's program where I met superstars like Steven Covy, Brian Tracy and Dr. Edward Demming - the American who taught the Japanese about quality. Deepak Chopra and Andrew Weil were among guests that I had the unbelievable experience of talking to personally.

The drive to the small town of Hammond, Louisiana, where Edwin's legends were made, would be little over an hour. His family's 400-acre plantation home sat about another 15 minutes down a country road on the river in Springfield. I had been lucky enough to be a guest frequently through the years, and I was just me ... not like the other famous individuals from around the world that Edwin knew. Suddenly, the challenge of finding someone to keep my four daughters went away. Without even a blink, the plane ticket to New Orleans was purchased. The glass was definitely half full ... the Bloody Mary glass, that is! I found myself choosing the best rental car money could buy – a brand new Ford Mustang convertible. "It's for Edwin," I thought. Crying hard? Might as well drive fast. Edwin would love this!" I thought.

It's not often that I get away to one of my favorite places like New Orleans - a city that Edwin, my staff, and his loved ones had shared. The service was not until tomorrow, and I had some "depression money" to spend ... in Edwin's honor, of course. I wandered the streets, buying art that was still wet and a pair of black leather cowboy boots. Later that evening, I arrived at my small hotel, dreading – yet pondering – how beautiful the service for a "man of thousands" would be. I wondered how many famous hairdressers and spa personalities would be there.

Sleeping soundly, awaking early enough, I found myself procrastinating...wanting to look just right for a man who I admired most for my entire 20-year career. I was going to be late for the 10 a.m. dedication! This bothered me, but I took comfort in the fact that Edwin would expect me to be late. He knew me better than anyone.

Margo Blue

82

The Gift
Keri Davis

Launching my career in the beauty business was an exciting time in my life. With my dad as my biggest supporter, I couldn't go wrong. My dad was my first client, (getting rid of his comb over was my first fete). He cried with every trophy I had ever received. When I turned 23, my world came tumbling down; my dad died suddenly of a heart attack. I felt lost; I couldn't even imagine what my life would be like.

Over the next few years of mourning, searching and finding hope, I found myself building amazing new relationships.

Today, my mom and I are best friends as well as business partners in a salon in San Diego. We have built a small 1000-square-foot salon into a million dollar a year business. We have the most amazing team who give themselves daily to make others feel beautiful. They help turn the frazzle days into calm, the sad days into serene and the un-pretty days into beautiful.

The gift that my dad left me, and continues to leave me, is to live up to my potential. Don't, not even for a minute, sell yourself short; "it" can always be better.

That's a blessing and a curse. The course of my father's life shaped and changed my life.

I can't say it is for the best, but I can say it has caused me to wake up and live the life I love – the life I was intended to have.

I used to drive myself hard to prove to my dad I could do it. Today, I do things for myself – knowing he is looking down as my biggest cheerleader.

There are no guarantees, only opportunities.

Beauty Tip: *You can't make everyone happy. Do things for yourself. If you can make yourself happy, you'll thrive in life.*

Keri Davis, President
keri@gilarut.com
www.gilarut.com

84

Live My Friend

Louie Aceves

I hear the whipping blades of a Huey helicopter, but where is it? "On Line!" That order is only given when you are going to find something or you are going to kill something. Who are they going to kill? Are we at war? Did I just get hit? Why can't I think? All these thoughts are racing through my mind. We are Recondo, the eyes and ears of the US Army. We live by our creed, "We leave no fallen comrade behind, no matter where or what the odds."

"Move out!" I must make my move now. With all my might, I push myself up and instantly feel unimaginable excruciating pain. I yell, "I'm hit," and continue to scream in agony!

"Over here!" The medic assures me that everything is fine. Within seconds, just like a slow-motion movie scene, I see myself being rushed to the Huey on a stretcher. This isn't the jungle. This is the middle of the freeway. What the hell is going on? From the helicopter I see what used to be a car. It's crushed like a pancake.

Several days later I awoke in the hospital. I was told the deadly accident had thrown me about 75 feet from the back-seat of our car. For the past 10 months, I had ridden "shot-gun." That morning, as a birthday honor, I let my friend take the seat. He died in my place when a mechanical failure took the car completely out of control and slammed us into a light post at 80 mph. We were only 19.

The Creator's most precious gift is life. What you do with your life is your gift to the Creator.

Using my life to create beauty is my inspiration. I have a license that allows me to touch people and care for them. Each day when my clients come to me they become a part of me. Like Merlin, the wizard with a license to touch, beauty makers go in and out of people's lives molding their beauty and inspiring their spirit. How we react to people when they are in our lives will determine how they react in their lives. If we do our

85

jobs to the best of our abilities, the client gives us the joy of knowing that we are the keepers of their trust and beauty.

When you trust someone you feel good. When you feel good, you look good. So what inspires me to do what I do? Vida, mi amigo, vida.

Beauty Tip: *Do you want to keep your eye make-up looking bombshell beautiful for hours? First, apply foundation for a good base coat. Next, apply a dusting of setting powder to your lids. The third step is to add your favorite eye colors. To lock in the look, you've created, dust the eyelids again with setting-powder.*

Louie Aceves
ariail@ez2.net

86

Your Personal Style
Steven and Annie Casciola

Style—it's everywhere. Everyone and everything has a personal style that defines who, or what, they are. At Salon City Star, our style is to be like a multi- faceted mirror, reflecting back to you a myriad of images and beliefs and stories. We are passionate about celebrating the beauty, truth, and goodness in our readers, in our industry, and in the world at large.

We believe that beautymakers are not just the ones who style your hair or set the latest fashion trends. Beautymakers are those who create and embrace beauty wherever they are, no matter the surrounding circumstances. They're the ones who rejoice in it, who support it, and who nurture it in others. They can be celebrities of the screen or stage, or famous industry professionals, or the least-known among us. But we write about all of them on our big slick pages and give you giant glossy pictures in brilliant colors because we want them (and us!) to be noticed.

Why? Because we believe that beauty, and those who create it, are worthy of your attention. Even more importantly, we believe that in your own unique style—and even if you don't yet realize it, that you are a beautymaker, too.

Sometimes it's hard to see the beauty in ourselves. If we're carrying a few extra pounds, if we can't afford the latest fashions, or if an unhappy heart is carried out to the world in a demeanor of despair, it can be difficult to see the beauty underneath it all. But it is there, just waiting to be discovered.

We want you to stand center stage in the world, to show us your style and to shine! Being willing to do that will take you a long way toward achieving your dreams. And that takes us to the featured beautymakers in this book, which is celebrating living a life of beauty. Within these pages you'll read about many of the beauty stars that exist around the country who really care about what we project as a new salon society and community of conscious professionals. Many of those featured

87

are behind-the-scenes stars who all deserve high marks for making people look and feel ravishingly beautiful – and truly cared about, day after day.

How do beautymakers do it? Read on. These are down-to-earth stories of individuals who made a choice to stand out and sprinkle stardust on other people's lives and careers.

We hope Salon City Star – and this book in particular – will give you the encouragement to find the beautymaker within and show it to the world. That's just our style.

Beauty Tip: *Knowing the chemistry between people is more important than knowing the chemistry in a bottle. Start being a beautymaker now. Tune into people. Be one with all. And when you meet someone, be the first to smile and say hi.*

Steven and Annie Casciola
www.saloncity.com
info@saloncity.com

88

No License Required

LaDonna Roye

As a hairdresser working in south Florida, many of my clients are retirees, and several are widows or widowers living alone.

The first Christmas I lived here one of my clients, Wilma, a widow, gave me a thoughtful gift. I said "thank you" and gave her a hug. She held on, hugged me back tightly, and said "Wow! That was the best hug I've had all day." She thought a moment and said, "That was the only hug I've had all day—all week—all month!"

I quickly realized that she wasn't kidding. I was the only person who had actually touched this lady in more than a month! Physical contact is something people crave – something babies die without!

Only three professions are licensed to touch other people, medical doctors, massage therapists, and cosmetologists. I touch my clients' hair, faces, necks and shoulders everyday in my work, but Wilma made me realize that a simple hug between two people touches both hearts… no license required.

Inner Beauty Tip: Smile! The corners of your mouth lift, your cheeks elevate, your forehead smoothes out, and your eyes sparkle. Its nature's face lift!

Beauty Tip: To remove hair product build-up: place a teaspoon of baking soda in the palm of your hand, add a small amount of shampoo, lather, rinse, repeat if necessary.

LaDonna Roye
wingoroye@comcast.net

89

90

August in India

Tiffany Miller

For a small town girl, "August in India" sounds like a book title. But for this Montana woman, it was real and completely life altering. Having only experienced the United States, India was an enlightenment of dramatic proportions.

After 30 hours of flying and numerous customs and immigrations checks, we arrived in Chennai, India. Stepping out of the air terminal I knew there was no turning back. Breathing was more like sucking in hot dirt and the smells were something all their own.

It wasn't long before I became accustomed to having a heavy coating of black soot in my nose and ears. Throughout the journey I thought that this fair skinned girl was finally getting a tan; too bad the tan washed away with a little soap and water.

Compared to the concrete jungles and gray skylines of most American airports, India was a welcomed contrast. The lush green hillsides with vibrant red-orange flowers gave way to a city rich in culture and hospitality. The friendships formed with the extraordinary spirits of India would prove to be the most valuable souvenir of this expedition. We set out on various adventures to places far and wide, saw incredible sights, but more importantly made memories of a lifetime.

Before leaving mundane routines and all things familiar stateside, my friend for the journey had given me some advice. He said, "Don't have any preconceived notions and keep an open mind." Often in India his words came back to help me make the transitions between cultures. Faded jeans and black t-shirts became bright yellow saris.

Stepping out of the world of runways, fashion models and surface beauty into a different setting was my awakening. Spending August in India enlightened me to the reality that we all have our own path to follow. Embarking upon it is half the battle and the transition is made easier by keeping an open mind.

Beauty Tip: *You don't have to travel to the other side of the globe to find new truths, new people and new friends. But you'll never go anywhere without the will to try and an open mind.*

Tiffany Miller

Sharing Inner Beauty

Karen Hardee

As a little girl I dreamed of being a hair designer. From a child's perspective, I thought of hairstyling as, "Just making everybody as pretty as they could possibly be."

When I grew up and made the dream a reality, I learned there was much more to it than that. Each day, I would touch people's lives in different ways.

Several years ago, one of my clients went through chemotherapy treatment, causing her to lose her hair. We ordered her a wig. When it arrived, she came in to have her head shaved. Until that night, my job had always been fairly easy. It seemed I worked effortlessly, relying on the gift God gave me. That night changed my life. I was forced to look beyond her hair and see my job for what it really was. It wasn't just making someone's hair look great, but making them feel great.

I managed to make her laugh and realize that "hair is just hair." It wasn't something that defined her worth. I told her to think about it as having a different hairstyle every day. I hugged her and gave her a kiss before she walked out the door. As I closed the door behind her, the tears streamed down my face. I thanked God for giving me the strength to do my job and help make her feel pretty again. I knew I couldn't fail her. She needed to feel good about herself during this most difficult time. And now she did.

As women, our hair means everything to us. Yet, it was at that precise moment I realized that, with our special gifts, we can make every person we touch see her real value. The person in our chair may be teetering on the edge, and we may be the only person they talk to that day. We can never forget: the person you touch may actually need more from you than perfect hair.

95

Beauty Tip: *Apply your styling product at your root area and when blow drying. Focus heat at the root area for maximum volume.*

Karen Hardee
khardee506@atmc.net

94

Life Is Good
Kelvin St. Pham

In 2000, I took a trip to the country of my birth, Vietnam. I said to my friend Oliver, as I looked at a little boy who was about the age I was when I left, "That could have been me at 6 years old!" Then I look at my nephew, who is about my age now, I said to myself, "That could be me right now." Wow!

I wouldn't be the person I am today if my family, were not somehow miraculously transported to America when I was 6 years old. For one, I would not be an American; I would be only Vietnamese. It's an honor to be born in Vietnam and to be a Vietnamese, but you know something, I'm a little bit of all my friends – a little black, a little brown, a little yellow, and even the "white man" has had an influence in my life. It's all good!

I have an amazing life; I've traveled to many beautiful places, England, Holland, Germany, Japan, Vietnam, Thailand, and Ireland (my favorite).

I'm now the owner of St. K Salon, a nail training salon and St. K Agency, a professional nail agency, where we're on the cutting edge of strictly quality nail services. We provide mobile nail services for many agencies in the Los Angeles area. We currently are providing nail services for Fred Segal Beauty in Santa Monica.

I'm also a Nail Educator for Creative Nail Design supporting the Asian nail market. I love making an impact on my fellow nail techs, in nails or in life.

Currently, I work with many celebrity clients on location for movies, videos, photo shoots and awards show. I've worked with Kylie Minogue, Jewel, Christina Aguilera, Pink, Gwen Stephani, and many others.

What a different life I would be living if my family would have stayed in Vietnam. I'm sure it will be great…but all I can say is…LIFE IS WONDERFUL!!!

Beauty Tip: *For healthy looking hands and nails, one should use a high quality hand lotion and deep pen-*

95

etrating cuticle oil like Solar Oil from Creative Nail Design. Use it daily and your hands and nails will always look beautiful, healthy, and, supple.

Kelvin St. Pham
St. K Salon/Agency
Owner
www.stkagency.com
info@stkagency.com

96

Making a Difference…One Haircut at a Time

Heidi Karnoscak

What difference could a hair designer make following the devastation of 9/11?

After 9/11, like so many people around the world, I was distressed and wanted to do something to help. As I talked with friends and clients and prayed, God spoke to my heart and showed me that I could fly to New York and cut hair for firemen. I called a firehouse in Queens and shared my plan to cut their hair to say thanks for all they had done for their fellow firefighters and community. So I packed up my tools and my products and set off for New York.

When I arrived at the firehouse there was a somber attitude all around, yet they greeted me warmly. Soon, they began lining up for their chance to have this crazy girl from California create a work of art on their heads! Some brought their wives and kids for a service. I cut, colored, gelled, highlighted and flat-topped. They loved their new looks.

We laughed, cried and connected as people do in the midst of tragedy.

It was then that I realized I could make a difference, one haircut at a time. I was able to serve 35 people from Engine 325, Ladder 163, in Queens, New York. One fireman needed to talk as he shared with me that two of his friends had been killed on 9/11 so I listened. Another guy showed me his locker where he had hung the fireman's prayer I had given him.

I realized I couldn't make their pain go away, but I could cut hair, listen and show compassion.

What we think may not be much, but when done with a servant's heart, it can be life changing and make an enormous difference for someone.

I went back the next year after hosting a cut-a-thon at my salon to raise money for the widows and orphans of that firehouse. We raised $3,000, and I delivered it. I was able to express

97

appreciation to them in that because of their dedication, we are a better nation of people.

I learned one small act of kindness can make a huge impact; one that will never be forgotten.

Love is spread and lives can be changed. What a difference a haircut makes.

Beauty Tip: *After you blow dry hair, mix gel and liquid shine together. Rub it into the hair to give hair lots of texture, shine and hold. You'll be amazed at the hold it gives!*

Heidi Karnoscak
heidi@inspiringchampions.com

98

Dream, Believe, Achieve!!

Andy Bodine

If you dream of something and believe it to be worthwhile and you are willing and able to take the action necessary, then it is certain that you will achieve it. "Dream, believe, achieve!" That's Norman Vincent Peale's positive prescription for life.

It all starts with desire! The desire to be or to do is the starting point for all achievement. Write down your dream in detail and think about it constantly. In doing this, you are actively making your dream into your goal. It must be in your thoughts every single day. Our subconscious mind is a very valuable tool, our actions will always follow our thoughts so whatever we think about consistently is what we will ultimately move towards.

The formula is simple: dream + belief + action = achievement. It has proven to be successful many times in my life. When I was 8 years-old, my mother took me to a salon in our small town. I can still remember the salon name: "Your Father's Mustache." As a child, I was intrigued by the salon experience. My stylist's name was Leon, and he was totally cool. He would always ask me, not my mother, how I wanted my hair done. Leon left such a positive impression on me, that I wanted to be a stylist just like him. I daydreamed about being a stylist someday.

Nine years later when I was finishing high school in the United Kingdom, I had a friend named Paul who was apprenticing in a London salon. Again I began to dream about becoming a stylist and I truly believed that I could do it. So I decided to take the final step: action!

That meant working full-time during the day and going to cosmetology school at night and on the weekends. It took four years and a lot of focus before I finally achieved my goal. Once I did, I was a licensed stylist off to a fantastic start of an amazing career.

Believe our cover when it says, *Wake Up…Live the Life You Love.* You can create your own destiny. Just always remem-

99

ber these words: If you can dream it and believe it, you can achieve it!

Beauty Tip: *To stay one step ahead of fashion and hair*
trends in the United States, pick up a copy of British
or Italian Vogue, the editorials will give you a
sneak peak of what's coming soon to America.

Andy Bodine
www.hairbybodine.com

100

Love is All You Need

Albie Mulcahy

I have learned very valuable lessons in my 28 years in the beauty business. One of the most important lessons I've learned is that both people and life are beautiful.

When I returned from Vietnam, I didn't have a clue what I wanted to do with my life. I worked at the post office, a variety of government jobs, and in factories, but I wasn't satisfied. One night, I went with a bunch of buddies to see the movie, *Shampoo*.

I was so inspired by the movie and the character played by Warren Beatty that I immediately signed up for beauty school. Within two weeks, most of my associates had dropped out, but I fell in love with the industry. I am still in love.

One of the most important lessons I have learned from my business experience is that nothing comes to you for free. You have to work hard and have a passion for what you do to get to the level you desire.

101

I really feel that my specialty is making people feel loved. When a person sits in my chair feeling upset, I put a lot of effort into making her feel beautiful, happy, and loved. I have witnessed dramatic transformations in my client's lives because of the love for what I do. I also try to pass my experience on to younger stylists. I enjoy working with young people because they want to learn so much. I never hesitate to put someone on the stage if they are a talented stylist, regardless of how new they may be to the business.

Why "pay your dues" when you don't have to?

My career as a stylist has brought me so much joy and fulfillment because I am doing what I love while making others happy and beautiful in the process. I dedicate this story to my daughter Veronica Jean Mulcahy who keeps me thinking like a child and gives me great tips on hair as well.

Beauty Tip: *Creativity is something we all are born with; not something that can be taught. It comes from within and can only bloom with intense love for yourself and the world around you. So hold on to your childhood dreams and the creativity will flow. For the last ten years, my most creative teacher has been my daughter, Veronica Jean Mulcahy, the love of my life and the one who keeps me thinking and believing like a child. She gives me great tips on hair, too.*

Albie Mulcahy
thevelvetlounge@aol.com

102

Feeling Like a Star
Mati Avidol

It's ironic how something as negative as a sister's illness can lead to something positive. My sister was a hairstylist and when she became sick, she couldn't continue to work full time. At her request, I came and helped her two days a week. Unfortunately, she became weaker and my two days working turned into seven. Later, when my sister's health improved, I was free to go back to my old job, but I realized I had no desire to return. In the salon, I found my true calling. Working there made me feel alive. I loved serving my customers one-on-one, and because of the rapport I built with them, business exploded!

Being attentive to my clients needs, I noticed that many of my clients were interested in wigs. Instead of sending them off to some wig store, I started researching how to make them myself! Every great endeavor begins with one small step, and I am proud to say we now make some of the most beautiful high-quality human-hair wigs available anywhere! Today, we have many faithful wig customers, some of whom you've seen in movies, TV, and even on the nightly news!

So here we are today, a wildly successful salon catering to the needs of the famous and the not so famous. Everyone who comes to Fuzzy Navel however, feels like a star! Our customers know that they will get want they want. If they want more hair than God gave them, it is possible. And, they will enjoy the process in a fun, unpretentious, friendly environment where they can really put their feet up and let their hair down.

Beauty Tip: *Treat yourself like a star every once in a while. Take a trip to the spa, massage therapist, or whatever makes you feel good. Take a friend with you. It is always better to share experiences than to live it all alone.*

Mati Avidol

In Beauty

104

Seeing the Beauty Within
Ana Beall

In many ways modern Albuquerque is still a frontier town; we still live with great wide open spaces. Because of this, we tend to need a look that is usually practical most of the week and fabulous only on Sunday. And every now and then a gang blows into town and sets the local sheriff on his heels making for a great old western gunfight!

I work from home, in a studio salon, yet I manage clients who want that spectacular look for a special occasion, or they have a need for a certain professional image, or they simply want to look their best most of the time. So, it's up to me to take what is in front of me and make it work.

Last year I worked on a photo shoot with a spectacular photographer, Don Campbell. We worked in my studio salon, and I selected several of my favorite clients as models. It was a fun-filled day of makeup and hair, food and drink, and the occasional trick of the trade to hide this flaw or bring out that wonderful feature. The girls were ecstatic, the photographer was happy as a beaver chewing tree trunk, and I was working like a maniac to get the girls done and in front of the camera. Madness! Mania! Euphoria!

I enjoyed when the girls' photos came up on the photographer's computer monitor and the girls were in awe of themselves as they looked at the beautiful woman on the screen; the woman I see when they walk into my little shop.

At the end of the day, exhausted and tired, Don and I were going over the more than 600 photos we had taken that day. We were happily patting ourselves on the back for a job well done and talking about how wonderful the girls had been when he says to me, "They sure don't look like that when they walk in!"

I told him, "Of course not, that's my job!"

I truly believe that it is my purpose to bring out the best in everyone who walks into my studio. Every person who walks through my door already has a color scheme, a form, a layout. I take what they have and make it into something more pleasing, something more inviting, and something more beautiful. That's my job: seeing the true beauty within!

Beauty Tip: *A good shampoo will work wonders in making your hair color remain true to tone between services. Most people run for a better conditioner when they are having trouble with dryness and color fading, not realizing that the problem is most likely caused by the harsh detergent in the shampoo. Hair is a fiber, and like a favorite sweater, repeated washings with a harsh detergent will cause the color to fade.*

Ana Beall
anabeall@msn.com

106

The Angel of Sleep
Frank Gruber

Five months after my father's death I was still having trouble sleeping – to the point of needing a doctor's help. One night, I remember staring at the clock for hours and getting only 2 ½ hours of sleep.

I wasn't really sure why I was experiencing sleeplessness. I didn't link it to my father's death. On the day he died, I was supposed to be playing golf with him. I had not imagined that I would never see him again. He was playing golf when he suddenly collapsed and died of a heart attack. I felt I was handling the grief very well, and I was not aware of any guilt.

Part of me was glad I wasn't there to witness his death, and another part wishes I could have been there. He wanted to spend more time with me and, because business was doing very well, I took Saturday's off to join him on the golf course.

The six weeks following my father's death, business was booming, but I was exhausted. I saw clients every half hour all day long while operating on four hours of sleep a night. One day I found an elderly woman sitting in my chair. I don't even recall how she got in my chair. I remember her smiling, looking at me and saying, "You look very tired."

Unexpectedly, I began telling her all about my trouble sleeping. She looked at me, smiled and said that my father forgives me, is proud of me and is in a really good place.

She told me to continue to work and live without any feelings of guilt about him. Her words immediately calmed me. I felt like a weight had been lifted.

My sleep returned to normal long before anyone ever brought it up again. When someone finally asked me how I had been sleeping, I told them that it had returned to normal ever since the mystery lady talked to me. I have not seen her since that day.

I did not catch her name and have no idea how to contact her. All I know is that her kind words comforted me and helped me come to peace with my father's death.

Frank Gruber
fgruber3@aol.com
Avante@avantesalon.com
www.avantesalon.com

Doors of Opportunity
Michele Allmon

Many people in the beauty industry are business owners or independent artists. In today's world, that can be intimidating. Success calls for vision and courage. I believe that when a door opens, you need to walk through it. Sometimes that door may not seem like the right opportunity, but you need to be able to dance in the moment and seize the magic when it happens.

I heard about a man who went from living in his car to being fabulously wealthy. When asked what made the difference, he said he was willing to take risks when they presented themselves even if they did not turn out for the best. I took that as a lesson in perseverance.

Some of the best experiences come from the hardest things we have to deal with. The scariest things can teach us the most, even when we do not want another lesson. This is where perseverance is essential. You have to stick with your goals and dreams even when life gets tough. You must also have the courage to accept failure when things don't work out. This means letting go of things that are not working for you. Move on to the next adventure.

One of the scariest doors that I had to walk through was deciding to have a family. That was a door that had been closed for a long time. I did not see children as an enhancement to my life. I was more focused on my own wants and desires. When I decided to bring children into my life, I learned that it was not a question of what I was going to be receiving but what I had to give.

Having children has humbled me and brought me so much joy. My children make me want to be a better person. I get so much more than I ever dreamed. These gifts would have never come to me unless I was willing to risk entering through the door of opportunity. Every day is not easy and some days are filled with headaches. It is on those days that we need to persevere, grow, and keep moving through the open doors.

Beauty Tip: *If you would like to have beautiful and well kept hair, and are wanting to grow it out get regular trims to keep your ends smooth, clean, and frizz free.*

Michele Allmon
www.awildhair.net

Find Your Beauty in the Dark
Jillian Alexander-Gregory

Where do you find your true beauty?

Look into the darkness. See yourself in the shadow of your forgotten self. Nurture and heal your unlovable side. Find yourself in the dark and you will truly find your light.

What makes you feel beautiful?

To walk in beauty is to bring your personal Truth, your heart's desires, out into the world and make your love visible. Let the wind whisper to your spirit. Listen as it says, "Yes, you are beautiful."

Ugliness is a worthy opponent.

Face the aspects in yourself or others you find to be repulsive. Use the energy as a chance to grow, rather than a place to judge. Take what you see and accept it, then use what you learn to transform it. Conquer your opponents and find your strength to live in balance.

The essence of beauty is a mystery.

See the fabric of the night sky as the shining stars are defined against the blackness. The darkness exalts their light. Find your essence in the sharp strike of a lightning bolt and the watery ocean mirror as the moon shines its phases on the surface. The brightest and the weakest stars all bring magnificence to one another. Look into the mirror of the eyes around you.

Search for yourself in the mirror.

Courageously radiate your light into the world. Sing your song of harmony into the night sky. Fearlessly heal the darkness you find there. Smash the mirror of illusion and find your truth in the reflection of your magnificence. Be the beauty you are looking for in the world. Live it out loud. This is what I already see in you. I stand as a witness to your truth and I find it breathtaking.

111

Beauty Tip: *Learn to live within the circumfer-*
ence of your polarities, and you will find whole-
ness. Find your beauty in the dark.

Jillian Alexander-Gregory
www.jagbeautyistruth.com
info@jagbeautyistruth.com

112

In Beauty

Angels Among Us
Monique Iacobacci

Beauty is in the eye of the beholder. In a field that caters to a predominantly female clientele, I feel it necessary to address beauty in all its forms, degrees, mysteries, and phenomenon.

I have seen physically beautiful women who not only lack inner beauty and confidence, but, most importantly, the ability to see everyday beauty that life has to offer.

Then there are our earthly angles; the women who light up the room, not only with their presence but also with one "not so perfect smile."

These women exude an inner beauty that is not evident to the naked eye. So what actually constitutes true beauty in an industry so obsessed with self? How can one technician make an impact in the ever-changing profession? My job is to try to convey a balance to these dilemmas.

There have been times when my professional calling has taken me far beyond the scope of my expertise into a realm where I am not only a beauty maker but a confidant. I have witnessed many important moments in people's lives: from battered woman to bachelorette parties, weddings to funerals, proms to pregnancies and every moment in between.

It saddens me that we judge based on our outer appearance. So, I decided to search out my own soul to find my inner-beauty. After all, it has been said, "to see the good in others, you must see the good in yourself." Every time I am faced with a situation that causes me to be a "life advisor" for my client, I am forced to reach within for answers. I have come to the conclusion that the real beauty in this industry is the relationship between the technician and the clients. It all boils down to these very important ideals:

Trust: to wholeheartedly place yourself under the guidance of someone else with your physical and emotional being.

Loyalty: to have an alliance with someone, to display faithfulness and confidence in each other.

Commitment: to each other; and to stay steadfast in the betterment of our selves, inside and out. All of these actions lead to one big phrase: TLC – love. This is the most important thing we can do for one another – to love one another, as we love ourselves. To search out one's soul and pull up the beauty that God has so deeply and firmly planted there, has a great reward. To truly see yourself and those around you, how God sees you, is the greatest gift a human can receive. For this, I am truly blessed.

"Be not forgetful to entertain strangers: for thereby some entertained angels unaware."
--Hebrews 13:2

Beauty Tip: *Always keep eye cream in the refrigerator to help reduce puffy eyes.*

Monique Iacobacci

114

The Business of Beauty

Robert Leonard

I love my work because my values are made real at the Robert Leonard Salon and Spa. I believe intimacy, love, and creative expression are the most important things in life.

When John Martin and I developed the salon 20 years ago, it was with the idea that positive and caring relationships with employees and customers are central to our spirit.

Our focus is as much about developing inner beauty as it is about creating outer beauty.

Everything I feel, think, and act upon is based on values of love and compassion. I was raised on a dairy farm in Missouri, and when I was a very young boy, one of my tasks was to care for young calves after birth. Nurturing calves during my formative years proved to be an important outlet and my saving grace. At a young age, I realized that people, too, must be shown tenderness and nurturing in order to thrive.

However, because I was a boy, I wasn't encouraged to demonstrate sensitivity and nurturing. I found a way around this taboo. My mother and sister allowed me to fix their hair. For me, this was the perfect way to express my love, and it was incredibly fun to watch as my talents transformed them. After our styling sessions they felt beautiful too.

So, at a very young age my goal was crystal clear: to create a marriage between my passions and intrinsic artistic expression.

I followed my passion and learned the art of styling. Opening the salon wasn't easy. John and I learned that opening a salon would call on business acumen that neither of us knew we had. But we held to our dream and focused on our goals. And, since the very first day, our values have not wavered. The spirit of Robert Leonard is about helping people to be the best they can be. Staying true to our beliefs and values, we have found personal and financial success.

Part of being the best is developing a positive image that is rooted in self-respect.

Embracing our bodies as amazing gifts from nature promotes this self-respect. So, the ultimate goal of the Robert Leonard Salon is to help each individual develop and project confidence.

I believe that true beauty lies in benevolent action. My craft allows me to live my values while being creative. That's why I love my work.

Beauty Tip: *I believe that inversion is the best way to maintain glowing skin. By inversion I mean literally being upside down; standing on your head, hanging from your knees or being in an inverted yoga pose. You see, it's something you must do for yourself: no one can do it to you or for you.*

Robert Leonard
info@robertleonard.net

116

A Fly On The Wall

Francie Ewing-Giles

I always looked at my job positively because I enjoyed my work, performed it to the best of my ability, and was able to pay my bills. Nevertheless, I still considered it to be a job, one of life's necessary evils.

My perspective changed immediately following the events of September 11.

Thanks to a conversation in my shop, I realized that "my job" was far more significant than I thought. It was far beyond that. It was about image enhancement for a lot of diverse, beautiful individuals who were seeking comfort, security and a place where their individuality could shine.

My enlightenment occurred as I happened to overhear a conversation between three clients in the waiting area on September 12, 2001. One of them said, "I'm sure glad these guys are staying open. It feels like my home away from home here. It's the only place where I can go and say or talk about anything I want to, and I know that nobody will think any differently of me. In a world of such ugliness, hatred and fear right now, this is my haven! When I walk through those front doors, I know they care about me. I know everyone is here because they want to look and feel beautiful and just forget about the outside world for a little while!"

This was the day I realized how important all people can be. What I do is obviously more than just a job. I had no idea that simply offering a listening ear can have an impact on someone else's life. I learned a great lesson about life enhancement, which only encourages me to try harder, reach farther, and to make a difference.

When we help others with their image enhancement, it enhances our lives as well.

Each time we improve ourselves, we take tiny steps toward making this world a more beautiful place to be.

Beauty Tip: *If you always do what you always did, then you'll always get what you always got. If you are not happy with a result you are getting, do something different. I challenge you to do one thing everyday to help someone else feel beautiful and positive towards life.*

Francie Ewing- Giles
francieg@qwest.net

118

Nadean

Diane Pawlowski

The first time I met Nadean Mattson, she was working at Grady's Deli. It was one of four storefronts on a main street in our lakeside community. Our salon, Details, was right next door.

Kevin and Pam Grady were the deli's owners. My husband Anthony and I shared the ups and downs of business with them and they became our friends. I still remember what a hot, still night it was when Kevin stopped by.

"I've been diagnosed with leukemia," he told me. Fortunately, he received a bone marrow transplant, but he had to spend a lot of time in isolation while his immune system rebuilt itself. For nine months, we watched Kevin, Pam and their two young children struggle.

They had to hire someone to help at the deli and found a high school girl, Nadean, who seemed as reliable as she was bright and effervescent. Soon Nadean, who graduated from high school a week into her job, was opening the deli in the morning, working the counter, making food and stocking the shelves. I remember thinking, "An angel must have sent her to the Gradys."

It was almost Christmas when the phone rang at our house. It was Pam. "Kevin died today," she said. My heart broke for the Gradys and for Nadean. What was going to happen to her now? I talked to Anthony, because I wanted to create a position for Nadean in our salon and he agreed to give her a chance.

Nadean helped out as a receptionist; she came in early, stayed late, hung up coats, cleaned, helped with inventory and did anything else that needed doing. Nadean thrived at our salon and decided to switch from her study of nursing to cosmetology. We helped her attend the Brown Institute of Cosmetology in Mentor.

Five years ago, she graduated and got her cosmetology license. At the salon, she worked next to me, and observed carefully how to do things. She noted word for word how I spoke with clients.

119

The little, energetic, dedicated pixie I remember from the deli is now a senior stylist and an educator at our salon, working with the Aveda Corporation and training our new apprentices. Her hairstyles have been pictured in national magazines and she has become one of our most sought-after stylists. Give good people a chance, and good things happen.

Beauty Tip: *Think of the position in which your hair stylist holds the blow dryer when they style your hair - in a downward position. Chances are, you hold the dryer pointing up. You'll get better control blowing down on your hair—and less frizz, too.*

Diane Pawlowski
info@detailsalon.com
detailsad@comcast.net

120

Touched

Frankie Cacciato

Here I am again at the airport, awaiting the plane ride to another Beauty Convention, one of a kind, a little more important than others. An Award Ceremony…who would ever think I would be the recipient of an award…a Beauty Award…an industry leader so they say.

Already 16 years to date have passed…A new wife Kathy, what a great wife and mother, 3 more children, Gina starting 1st grade wow do you believe it – Sarah a teenager, man is she gorgeous, Rocko he's me looking in the mirror just like the old man, Frankie Boy a musician Excalibur and the terror of them all – still my sweetie Lauren. Two grand kids later boy, she's the leader of the pack and quite the topic of conversation both her and Frankie on that day when "it" happened.

Broken down really at that time no where to go but up, Divorced, living above a car wash in the attic, tons of financial headaches from walking out on my business, seeing a priest out in Indiana, counseling he called it and a heart that I thought would be un-repairable.

After months of being sick, just about at times ready to write off life, my close friend set me up for an interview – an interview for a job that would change the destiny of my life forever…

A design or you might say exhibit design house. Working with displays, graphics etc… So many things none of which I thought bearing only a High School Diploma would mean one bit of whatever to me. I met the owner, a young man that came off as being very business like and mature, a very detailed entrepreneur who fooled me for quite some time until "that day". I came on for really nothing, eventually moving out of the attic and into his home. That was a part of my "perk" a place to live; his car to drive and always a quite reminder of were the above came from.

121

Learning the trade, the people for which it services and working with a sales team for which I was destined to lead. Some travel, first hand education and some hardships still followed but I prevailed and did eventually learn not only the trade, all of which it offered but finally inherited the sales team from which my story truly begins...

My team, I thought the strongest of the strong fell short of my expectations one day when three visitors appeared at our door. One of great majesty, an "afro" hair style of sorts, beard, a wild outfit escorted by another fella, very bubbly, round glasses, ascot and a certain bouncy flair and the hottest escort of all, she had spiked heels, fishnet stockings, tiger skin outfit and with him along with everyone of my staff heading for the bathroom door were I was held up "so you can say". The banging on the door alerted me to a problem – come on out you gotta see these guys – well at least we think! Hurry up we aren't going by them!

What could it be? Who could they be? I was expecting "ski masks and guns a blazing". Now how foolish – 3 normal folks, 2 guys and a gal, Gee after what I have gone through, they looked pretty normal to me...actually GREAT!

Well two and a half hours went by in our office – we talked about my life, Lauren and Frankie Boy, my losses and my dreams... on and on... never once speaking of themselves or what they wanted. The majestic one of the three acting as if he knew me for years, well he said it's time to go – getting up, hugging and kissing goodbye and then he says "tell the kids they'll be O.K. their dad is just fine". It will all work out he said, you and I were destined to be together, your life will change, "a good man with a great heart" he boasted. "We'll all live on my Island one day"...while they headed for the door for a moment I was totally dumb founded, something that doesn't happen too often for me. "Wait" I yelled, "what was it you guys wanted? I don't even have a card or phone number to call you". With that in a hearty voice he began to laugh and said "I'll call

122

you, you've got just what we need...my name is Xenon, we are in the beauty business!"

Months and years have passed and also my dear friend... I thought an angel, a hairdresser by trade, platform artist, educator-teacher, school owner what a pro. We did so many projects together, shows, dinners and events.

A hairdresser...a hairdresser blessed with a talent that so many have, a gift to perform, an art, a trade, a gift to listen, a gift to care and a gift to give someone like me and so many others the time of day. What a special day that was for me...

Wheels up – I'm on my way...what a character, he helped me with the business that my wife and I are blessed with, introduced me to so many and helped me start a new career. Cosmetology...who would ever think? Then there is his wish... take care of my kids he always said. His students, his industry, future kids (he called them no matter what their age) that have the gift he had, to cut hair, to put on make-up, to educate, to do pedicures, to perform on stage..."take care of my kids and give them a chance!"

It's payback time...it's done – The Xenon Foundation, a dream come true to take care of his kids. Thanks my good friend – I'm touched!

Beauty Tip: *Take time out of your busy schedule to touch someone's life. No matter how small, it will be appreciated. You might never know how far it went.*

Frankie Cacciato

124

Healing Through Giving Others a Second Chance
Gabriel Choy

Why do I like being a photographer? Not just because I love creating beautiful images, but through photography, I have the opportunity to meet people from all walks of life.

Last year, I met Catherine, who was in her late 30's, at a fashion show, where she worked as a runway model for the very first time. We met up a week later so I could show her the photos I took from the event. While I was showing her the photos, we also shared stories of our past.

She received her cosmetology license when she was 18, a bachelor degree in psychology and in human growth and development, and has a 12- year-old son name Brandon. But as I continued to listen to her life story, I realized getting and giving a second chance in life isn't all that impossible.

When Catherine was very young, her mother passed away. She lived with her dad, who mentally and physically abused her. By age 12, she ran away from home—hoping to seek a better life. After a few months of being on her own, Catherine missed having a family. So she went to the state and asked to be placed in a foster home program. Little did she know, it wasn't everything that she hoped.

Catherine moved from one foster home to another every 30 to 90 days, usually sharing one bedroom with, sometimes, six to eight other foster kids, and had only a milk crate to store her belongings. Often times when Catherine moved into a new foster home, she would get sprayed by DDT, as part of the "sanitizing" procedure. Between foster homes, she would live on the streets, in abandoned warehouses, alleys, homeless shelters, and with complete strangers. As she was constantly moving from one place to another, it was difficult for her to find a sense belonging, and she developed a low self-esteem. As a result, she started to blame herself for everything that was wrong in life and she carried that feeling into her adult life.

When her six-year marriage failed with a man who had a great job, lived a lavish lifestyle and provided her with a strong

125

sense of financial security and emotional stability, she blamed it on herself even though he had been cheating on her with countless prostitutes and was charged for solicitation.

After the divorce, she went into a depression and felt completely lost in life. When she was at the lowest point in her life, fate gave her a chance to turn things around. After inheriting some money from her grandmother, she bought a condo for her and her son, across the street from an all-girls foster home. Instead of turning around and hiding from her emotionally-charged past, she decided to share her experience as a teen runaway and foster child, and provide emotional support to these girls. Even though spending time with these girls brought back many unpleasant feelings, Catherine continued her outreach because she doesn't want other foster teens to go through what she had been through.

Now at the age of 40, divorced, a single mother, with no retirement plan in place, and diagnosed with Interstitial Cystitis, a chronic inflammatory condition of the bladder wall, she actively volunteers for a local non-profit foster care agency. In addition, she aspires to become a social worker for the foster care system, for a private organization and create a 12-step support program for adults who were foster children once like her.

Instead of letting her experience as a foster care child hold her back from life, Catherine is now going full-force forward in giving other foster children a second chance.

* The real name has been changed in this story to protect the identity of the person.

Beauty Tip: *Dark circles under the eyes are often related to "toxicity" in the body. Detoxification of the body, especially the liver, could be helpful. I understand there are other quicker, instant solutions for this problem, but many are only temporary. This is not an overnight project. But if you work at it, stay with it, then there is a good chance you will be successful and have a very long lasting effect.*

Gabriel Choy
www.Gobofoto.com
Gabe@gobofoto.com

For your free gift, go to: **www.wakeupand.com**

Inspiration for Generations
Tommy Aucoin

A long time ago, before I was a hairdresser, a man I admired very much told me that I could be anything that I wanted to be and that I could do anything that I wanted to do, as long as I would "think positive, believe in myself and never ever quit."

I repeated his words to myself every time I was challenged or ran into adversity. Every time I pushed myself to reach further for my dreams I heard his voice.

This man was my dad, Lacey Aucoin. He was an extremely hard working middle-income man that worked long and hard to give his five kids the best education and life that he possibly could.

I remember the day that I told him I was going to be a hairdresser. He was stunned, not knowing what to say and finally he said, "What, are you sure, are you O.K.?" I said, "Yes, Dad, I'm going to create art, and people will give me money." He thought I was nuts but he said, "O.K. then think positive and be the best hairdresser that you can be and never give up."

He really thought I was nuts when I showed him an extremely avant garde magazine called *Oro Vision*, published in the 1980s. It was quite over-the-top styles created by big names in hairdressing. I showed him pictures of work from Mr. Irvine Rusk, a Scottish artist known all over the world for his haircutting, and told him that one day I would cut hair with Mr. Rusk. He said "O.K. son whatever you say, good positive thinking."

My dad saw me style hair in a salon with four friends. Later, it grew to 30 employees reaching the million dollar mark back in the 1980s. We created art and people gave us money. And he told me, "Never stop and always think positive and I would be whatever I wanted to be."

Unfortunately, my father became ill. He was diagnosed with colon cancer and given six months to live but lived three years because he never stopped thinking positive and believing in himself. My dad died at only 54 years-old.

127

He never saw me become the first American to cut side-by-side on a platform stage with Mr. Irvine Rusk.

He never saw me own or partner five salons and open Atelier Aucoin, my very own Advanced Training Academy.

He never met my beautiful wife, Jodi, and my beautiful, amazing son, Armond.

But every day I repeat his words in my mind and in my heart, "Always think positive, and never stop trying, and I can be anything that I want to be."

Now every day I tell my son, "Armond, believe in yourself, think positively and never, ever give up." I also tell him 12 times a day that I love him very much.

I wish I could say that to my dad today because I fear I never told him enough.

So live by this mantra, "Always think positively, always believe in yourself, never ever stop trying, and you will achieve whatever you desire."

Oh yes, and tell someone today that you love them very much, because we all need to know that we are loved.

Beauty Tip: *Pick your hairdresser wisely. Let his or her work be the deciding factor not price. Then have trust and respect for their training and listen to them. If you picked wisely you will realize all your style dreams.*

Tommy Aucoin
atelieraucoin.com
info@atelieraucoin.com

128

Style

Lee Beard

"Is this a good color to go with my hair?" He held the freshly-laundered shirt up next to his face.

The answer was obvious: he had no hair to speak of, and what little vestigial mane remaining was snowy white. So was the shirt.

"Perfect match," she said, quietly. It was an old joke, but she never tired of it. He had first used it over 30 years before when his forehead began its retreat toward the nape of his neck. Now, it was not so much a clever joke as it was a ritual.

They were off to church for a special program on missions. Someone (she could not quite remember who) was coming to talk about the work their church sponsored in India. That's why her husband would be unusually white-shirted tonight.

That's why he grumbled, too. "It just strikes me that we have enough heathens running loose in the county without having to go bothering someone else's heathens," he observed. Of course, if there had been another reason for going, he would have objected to that, too, on some other ground. Even after 15 years of retirement, he still resented using evenings for anything other than resting or recreation. Church going was, in his opinion, neither of those things.

After a short and, she thought, very interesting talk, she helped serve tea and other refreshments in the parlor. The little man from India, whose name she feared she could never pronounce, was very gracious.

She found his hint of a British accent made him seem wise and, in a way, mysterious.

People started to leave and she began her ritual of cleaning up. It was the habit of a lifetime; as messes were made, it was her instinct to eliminate them. The room was almost empty when she picked up a half-filled cup of tea only to hear a soft voice say, "Please."

She was face to face with the Indian visitor. "Please." He said, again, and she understood that he wasn't quite finished. She handed over the cup. "Oh," she said. "I'm sorry."

129

"There is no need, I assure you," he said, smiling. "Who are you, please?"

She smiled, gave him her name, and extended a hand.

"Yes," he said. "I did not ask your name, however. Who are you?"

She was instantly disoriented. She blushed, as if she had said something wrong. "Well, I'm on the hospitality committee," she said, as if having to explain her existence.

"I'm quite sure," he smiled. "But, who are you?" His question had a certain insistence.

"She is the most wonderful wife any man ever had, or could ever hope to have on this earth," said her husband as he eased up beside her and put a protective arm around her shoulder. He reached for the Indian's hand and introduced himself.

"Then I am the person who is shaking the hand of the world's most fortunate man," grinned the visitor, and everyone laughed. From thin air a committee descended and he was whisked away.

Later, in bed, she found she could not be comfortable. The little man's question kept nagging at her: "Who are you?" If not a name, if not a member of a group, then what answer could she give? Who was she?

She had not noticed that, earlier that night, she had been gliding around the room quietly looking after everyone else. There was a natural grace to the way she did it; a quiet evidence that concern for others lay at the very core of her being. She was not detached, but involved; not passive, but calm.

All those little things made a foreign visitor interested in her as a person – not as a set of classifications.

Her very being was reflected in the way she bore herself, and the things she did.

It was her style, and she didn't even notice it.

Such is the way with style. True style is not a function of whimsy or fashion. It is a manifestation of who and what we really are at the center of our beings. You cannot buy it, or wear it, and no one can give it to you.

People, houses, neighborhoods, even towns and cities have style. It has to do not so much with what you do, or what you have, but with what you dream or believe or remember.

And it is style – not fashion – to which people are always attracted. Fashion is a part of style, to be sure, but it is no substitute. What is your style? What is ours? For we are all in this together.

Her husband moved next to her. "Can't sleep?" he asked.

"I'm just wondering who I am," she said. "I mean, beyond a name and an address, who?"

He settled into his pillow. "That would take too long," he mumbled, "So I'm going back to sleep. And if it turns out you're not my wife, let's keep this a secret."

She smiled, and tolerated him. It was her style, after all, to do so.

Beauty Tip: *A sense of style comes from within. Don't worry about adopting the style of the time until you understand yourself and what makes you comfortable when you're among others. That's your style.*

Lee Beard
husband of Linda, "the world's most fortunate man"
lee@wakeuplive.com

131

132

Inspired Succes

Deedee Carlson

I didn't set out to own a beauty school but always knew I would be an entrepreneur. I just wasn't sure of what.

The beauty industry is fascinating and I have always found it interesting. However, my parents were set on college and participating in activities where "looks" didn't matter. Traditional education was foremost in their plan for their eldest daughter.

So I went to college, rowed varsity crew, took my first job at a thoroughbred racetrack as a marketing assistant where I was promoted to promotions manager, then sold corporate accounts on the benefits of Kinko's, but the entire time I plotted my future unknown business. I looked into Quizno's franchises, thought about being a wedding planner and settled on owning a day spa. I liked going to the spa, I know the difference between a good and a bad service, why shouldn't I just open my own? (I know now how naïve that was.)

At 26 I signed up at a local beauty school. The idea was, get my license, learn the business, work for someone else and then open my spa. It seemed simple enough.

Beauty school was a unique experience. You work 40 hours a week for five months meeting people one day and working six inches from their face the next. It was all about clocking hours and getting operations. It was nothing like working in a spa or salon.

A new spa was opening in my neighborhood. The word was that it was going to be the best in the city. I convinced the manager of the spa at the time to let me answer phones at the front desk while I was in school. Once I was licensed I moved to the treatment room. I was making more money working six hours a day at the beauty school than I did right out of college. I went to beauty school for five months, found a job, and was making great money with an 8 a.m. to 2 p.m. schedule in a fabulous environment. The best kept secret about the beauty business is that everyone is happy to see you. No one is ever in a bad mood

133

to see their esthetician, nail tech or hairdresser. I had made more money with Kinko's, but as an esthetician I was sleeping better at night. Plus, I wasn't taking my work home with me.

I continued to work on my business plan, carefully watching how management found the best spa technicians. This was a new multimillion dollar spa having difficulties, how was I going to get anyone to work for me? Everyone out of school needed to be an assistant or have more training, and then it hit me. San Francisco needed another school before it needed another day spa.

I called my former beauty school instructor (who had moved on from teaching) and started plans for the San Francisco Institute of Esthetics and Cosmetology.

I thought, "I'll keep going until someone says, "Stop!" Next thing I knew I was meeting people who wanted to be instructors and potential students. I remember talking to a co-worker (and now our admissions leader), "What if no one signs up? What if my perception of what school could be is not what the market demands?" SFIEC opened July 9, 2002 with nine students. I am glad that I never took my doubts seriously.

For the first time I felt that what I was doing was making a difference. We have people entering school ranging ages from 18 to 56 with diverse backgrounds and different motivations for coming to school.

Even after being featured on television and in industry magazines, I never stopped to enjoy the success. It hit me when a SFIEC graduate called and left me a message saying she was booked for the next two weeks. Seven months before she was a marketing manager, and now, she was a licensed esthetician running her own business and booked solid for two weeks. It was a reality check. Following my dream and starting this business is making it possible for others to do the same.

That's what keeps me inspired; I love being part of their success.

Deedee Carlson

Beauty Tip: *If you find it in your heart to care for somebody else, you will have succeeded.* —Maya Angelou

Beauty Begins Within
Mirror-Mirror on the Wall, Why Am I Asking You?

Jeffrey Paul

" 'It's nice to see you!' I said. 'It's nice to be seen!' She replied." —From The Saga of Eddie Sandler

It's interesting that we need to know that we are seen as beautiful in order to see and feel that way. The wicked queen in Snow White needed reassurance from an outside party. Few of us questioned why she had to ask. The concept of how we appear to others has a direct effect on most of us when it comes to seeing ourselves.

Psychologists tell us that there are three image concepts that strongly affect how we ultimately see ourselves: the way we see ourselves at the start; the way others see us; and the ways we think others see us.

Most humans criticize their appearance. After all, we are our own harshest critics. People tend to listen to their inner critics and begin doubting themselves – even if the people they see in the mirror are indeed beautiful. Their perception becomes distorted, and they no longer see is in the mirror – they see themselves as less than they really are.

Many of us heard our mothers telling us early in life that the way we see ourselves has a big impact on how others see us. As we age, we learn this to be true. So what you think about yourself is an important factor in the appearance you present – both to yourself and to others.

Earlier in my career, I worked with many beautiful models at magazine photo shoots and runway fashion shows. What struck me most about these stunning men and women was their need for constant reassurance about their appearance. Just like the rest of us, without reassurance, their anxiety affected the way they looked, and when they felt confident about their appearance, they projected that feeling effortlessly. Before my eyes, these

135

ordinary people transformed themselves into dynamic, radiant figures. What a difference a thought can make!

FLIPPED: A REAL-LIFE TURN-AROUND

The following story is a journey from "caterpillar" to "butterfly" and the metamorphosis of a lifetime.

Just three days before Gwen's 60th birthday, a coworker told her to get a face-lift. She stood up in front of our colleagues and said, "Can you believe we're just three years apart in age? Look at all her wrinkles!"

You can instantly imagine how this made Gwen feel. "My self-esteem was down in the dumps," she said. "I didn't want to be victimized by the aging process.'

Gwen was all too familiar with feeling like a victim, having experienced ongoing verbal abuse from the time she was young. "My mother told me no man would want to take me out during the daylight because of how I looked," she remembered. This message was reinforced when a teacher told Gwen, "Get a good education, because no man is going to want you."

After a lifetime of living with a low self-image, her coworker's statement was the last straw. Gwen decided to take action. "I read an article of Jeffrey Paul's on taking a Total Approach to image and well being. I thought to myself, 'This is what I need.' I needed to change my base, so that I could be grounded in something good. When I went to see Jeffrey, my spirit was broken. The warmth and love in that center not only helped me work on the outer things, but on my spiritual and emotional well being, too."

Gwen's outward transformation began with her hair. "My hair was thin and damaged and the longest it had ever been," she said. "Jeff consulted with me about the best design for my face and then a stylist cut my hair just as he prescribed. It was the most wonderful hairstyle, which was the beginning of a change for me."

The treatments Gwen began receiving regularly made a remarkable difference. Between the laser light therapy sessions that fortified her scalp, the botanical supplements that nourished her hair, and the high quality hair care products she began to use, within a few weeks she began to show a healthier, thicker growth of hair than she had ever imagined.

A week after her first consultation, Gwen returned for a facial, learned about skin care, and treated herself to a massage. "To my mother's generation, this would have been considered selfish, but it makes me feel as if I am blooming from a secret garden within. I'm finding that I am not slinking around being invisible anymore."

Determined to support herself on every level, Gwen scheduled a cosmetic makeover and a nutrition consultation to help her lose weight.

Experiencing how rewarding it could be to treat herself better, Gwen decided her own opinion is what counted. She found herself making choices that reflected her new realization.

Now well on the road to a more fulfilling and healthier lifestyle, Gwen hopes her story will inspire women of all ages. "I don't want others to experience the pain I did before seeking help. It's important to take charge of the way you look and feel. It has truly been a life-affirming experience for me."

"It's not what you look at that matters, it's what you see."
—Henry David Thoreau.

Jeffery Paul

AUTHOR INDEX

140

Chapman, Vision
Page 47

Owner, Christian's Visions
c/o C Visions Salon
8321 160th Ave NE
Redmond WA 98052
786-276-9344
www.seattlemodel.com
christian@seattlemodel.com
noboundaries3@aol.com

Choy, Gabriel
Page 125

206-679-4584
Owner/Producer Seattle International Fashion Week
www.sifashion.com
Gabe@gobofoto.com
www.Gobofoto.com
Seattle, Washington

Council, Van
Page 15

404-250-3356
www.vanmichael.com
reeve@vanmichael.com
Van Michael Salon
5505 Roswell Rd
Atlanta, GA 30342

Cox, Dwight
Page 53

Bella Capelli Hair Salon
110 E Tuscaloosa St.
Florence, AL 35630
256-765-9911

Cromeans, Robert
Page 19

619-559-8912
www.robertcromeans.com

Davis, Keri
Page 83

President, Gila Rut Salon
619-299-5750
keri@gilarut.com
www.gilarut.com
1010 University Ave. Ste. C213
San Diego, California 92103

Durocher, Bryan
Page 13

Success Coach
2000 Ponce de Leon Blvd. 6th Floor
Coral Gables, FL. 33134
Phone: 305-667-5870
Toll Free: 877-596-0243
www.durocherenterprises.com

Duvall, Scott
Page 35

503 238-4428
fotografatadaduv@qwest.net
Fotografata da Duvall Inc.
2025 SE 50th Ave.
Portland,Oregon 97215

141

For your free gift, go to: **www.wakeupand.com**

Ewing-Giles, Francie

(801) 972-1199 Fax (801) 972-4811
francieg@qwest.net
Salon Francesca, Inc.
1426 W. 3500 S.
Salt Lake City, Utah, 84119

Ferguson, Nancy

Freelance Stylist (Hair, Makeup, Fashion),
Consultant, Educator
P.O. Box 82934
Portland, Oregon 97282

Figueroa, Jose

Owner, Salon Jose
858-456-7279
jose@salonjose.com
7760 Fay Avenue
La Jolla, CA 92037

Fisher, Eric

Owner, Eric Fisher Salon
ericfishersalon@cox.net

Freddi, Chris and Angie

Owners, Avida Salon and Spa
915-592-4324
915-857-2442 fax
cfreddi@aol.com
www.avidasalon.com
1891 Lee Trevino Ste.900
El Paso, TX

142

Garlinger, Jamea

jamea@sbcglobal.net
Progressive Image Hair Art
Sacramento, California 91814
(916)444-3533

Gartland, Lauren

Founder & President of Inspiring Champions
619-280-5070, ext. 11
www.inspiringchampions.com
Lauren@inspiringchampions.com

Gerard, Gary

President
Gerard's International Advanced Haircutting Seminars
Tel 415-441-1156
Fax 415-441-9686
gerards@earthlink.net
www.GaryGerard.com
2519 Van Ness Avenue
San Francisco, CA 94109

Gruber, Frank
Page 107

fgruber3@aol.com orAvante@avantesalon.com
www.avantesalon.com
700 Downingtown Pike
West Chester, PA 19380
610-429-1800

Frank Gruber has been a salon owner for 25 years. He opened his first salon, The Klip Joint, in December 5, 1978 and opened his 2nd salon, Avante Salon & Spa, on October 1, 1991. He is now the co-owner of Euphoria Salon & Spa which opened August 1, 1998. Frank Gruber was one of the original board members of TSA and has been a consultant in the beauty industry for more than 12 years working with salon owners throughout the country.

Hall, Michael
Page 3

Platform Artist
Creative Director
HairLounge and Spa Salon
253-941-3680
Seattle, WA
www.fashionrocket.biz
michael@fashionrocket.biz

Industry Consultant for Wake-Up Live the Life You Love In Beauty District and Vice Chapter Leader for Soka Gakkai International–USA Co-trained and coached an international gymnastic team for SGI-USA, that have two entries in the *Guinness Book of World Records* Black Belt Rank in the Martial Arts

143

Hardee, Karen
Page 93

Co-owner, Totally Chic Salon & Spa
910-579-1035
khardee506@atmc.net
9188 Beach Dr SW
Calabash NC 28467

Hunt, Brenda
Page 75

Salon Owner/Administrative Director,
Panache Hair Salon and Day Spa
908-534-1512
brenda@panachespa.com
www.panachespa.com
Whitehouse Station, NJ 08889

Iacobacci, Monique
Page 113

Alexis7774@aol.com
973-800-9247

Karnoscak, Heidi
Page 97

Inspiring Champions
heidi@inspiringchampions.com
5694 Mission Center Road, #273
San Diego, CA 92108

Keane, Daniel
Page 41

Owner, Marketplace Salon
206-244-8886
djkeane32@hotmail.com
Burien, WA

144

Paul, Jeffrey
Page 135

Jeffrey Paul Beautiful Hair Center
21330 Center Ridge Road
Rocky River, Ohio 44116
W - 440-333-8939
F - 440-333-0200
C - 440-821-7500
lookurself@aol.com

Pawlowski, Diane
Page 119

Details Salon and Spa
20140 Detroit Road
Rocky River, OH 44116
440-333-9696
info@detailsalon.com
detailsad@comcast.net

Hair stylist and salon owner 16 years. Top 200 salon 4 years
in a row Salon Today Magazine. Has done hair and make-
up on 2 of the 3 Tenors. Nationally published hairstyles.

Picard, Helene
Page 61

Cosmetologist of 25 yrs
Published hairstyles
Runway hair
Competition winner
Owner
Hair Connoisseurs Salon & Spa
www.hairconnoisseurs.com
helene@hairconnoisseurs.com

145

Ponce, Evarista
Page 79

evarista@earthlink.net

Rohlfing, Rodney
Page 43

P.O. Box 46
Willisville, IL 62997
618-497-2801

Roye, LaDonna
Page 89

Salon Owner/ Success Coach
Hair Biz
931 Creech Rd
Naples, FL 34103
Phone: 239-434-8073
239-598-5007
wingoroye@comcast.net

Sanders, Jack
Page 57

President/Director, Technical Artistry
jack@techartsalon.com
www.techartsalon.com

146

For your free gift, go to: **www.wakeupand.com**